ANYONE CAN
PLAY MUSIC

ANYONE CAN PLAY MUSIC

Unlock Your Musical Potential
with the Laws of Brainjo

JOSH TURKNETT

A TarcherPerigee Book

tarcherperigee

an imprint of Penguin Random House LLC
1745 Broadway, New York, NY 10019
penguinrandomhouse.com

First self-published in the United States as *The Laws of Brainjo* by the author,
in 2020.

TarcherPerigee with tp colophon is a registered trademark of
Penguin Random House LLC.

Library of Congress Cataloging-in-Publication Data

Names: Turknett, Josh, author.
Title: Anyone can play music: unlock your musical potential
with the laws of brainjo / Josh Turknett.
Description: New York: TarcherPerigee, 2025. |
Identifiers: LCCN 2024033332 (print) | LCCN 2024033333 (ebook) |
ISBN 9780593850978 (trade paperback) | ISBN 9780593850985 (epub)
Subjects: LCSH: Musical instruments—Instruction and study. |
Music—Instruction and study—Psychological aspects. |
Music—Performance—Psychological aspects. | Practicing (Music)
Classification: LCC MT170 .T87 2025 (print) | LCC MT170 (ebook) |
DDC 784.071—dc23/eng/20240723
LC record available at https://lccn.loc.gov/2024033332
LC ebook record available at https://lccn.loc.gov/2024033333

Printed in the United States of America
1st Printing

Book design by Angie Boutin

The authorized representative in the EU for product safety and compliance is
Penguin Random House Ireland, Morrison Chambers, 32 Nassau Street,
Dublin D02 YH68, Ireland, https://eu-contact.penguin.ie.

For my coaches—Dr. James O'Donnell and Rob Bentley—
who taught me the "growth mindset" long before it was cool.

For my neurology mentors—Dr. Edward Valenstein,
Dr. Steven Nadeau, and Dr. Kenneth Heilman—
who taught me how to think about the brain.
And for all the supporters of Brainjo who are now
making music they never thought possible.

"Whether you think you can or you think you can't, you're right."
—HENRY FORD

"If people knew how hard I had to work to gain my mastery,
it would not seem so wonderful at all."
—MICHELANGELO

"All things are difficult before they are easy."
—THOMAS FULLER

"In a world where information is abundant and easy to access,
the real advantage is knowing where to focus."
—JAMES CLEAR

CONTENTS

ORIGIN STORY

. . . .

Dear Reader,

Growing up, I loved playing sports. Basketball and baseball were my first loves, then came tennis.

And I practiced. A lot. I loved practicing more than competing, in fact.

I shot free throws and three-pointers for hours, virtually every single day, no matter the weather. I wouldn't go inside until I hit at least ten free throws in a row (I'd heard Larry Bird did something similar, so I figured he was a pretty good example to follow).

I'd beg my brother, my dad, my babysitter, or just about any warm body I could find to play catch with me. Or hit me ground balls.

In retrospect, I realize now that I was thoroughly and utterly addicted to the learning process (still am). Getting better at things was the greatest fun imaginable. It felt like magic (still does).

And as far as I could tell, there was no limit to what you could get good at if you were willing to put in the time and energy. Every bit of evidence indicated that there was a direct correlation between how much I practiced and how much better I got.

But here's the strange thing. When I'd receive a sports-related compliment from the adults in my life, they were always something like:

"You're a natural shooter."

"You've got a great arm. Did your dad play baseball?"

"You've got a great eye."

A natural shooter? The first five hundred times I shot a basketball, I'd missed the rim entirely!

A great eye? The first fly ball I tried to catch thwacked me square in the forehead.

But based on what the grown-ups were saying, I was apparently born with these abilities. They were all inherited, written into my genetic code.

And those thousands upon thousands of hours of obsessive practice? Apparently superfluous. According to conventional wisdom, I practiced *because* I was good at those things, not the other way around.

Nobody ever said, *"Wow, you must practice a lot!"*

This never sat well with me. The idea that talent was innate seemed totally wrong and was entirely at odds with my firsthand experience.

I wasn't good at any of these things initially. Terrible, in fact. Just like everyone else I'd ever seen.

Practicing was what seemed to make all the difference. And not just how much I practiced, but *how* I practiced, too. Quantity *and* quality mattered.

I knew, deep in my bones, that the innate talent story was

wrong. I knew that my abilities weren't because of anything special about me but because of the path that I'd taken in acquiring them. And I knew that anyone else who followed that path could achieve similar results.

It seemed like there was a mass cultural delusion when it came to our beliefs about talent and ability. And those beliefs were limiting the potential of every human who held them (and, via the Pygmalion effect, those around them, too!).

At first, I just found all this confusing. But as time went on, it bothered me more and more. A seed was planted early on in my mind that, one day, I wanted to help stamp out this myth.

As I began a career in the neurosciences, I discovered the scientific explanations that refuted the delusion. All brains possess the same mechanisms for learning that allow us to master anything, from tennis to trigonometry. The human brain remains plastic throughout our lifespan, which means we can indeed learn new things and acquire high levels of expertise at any age. Whether we are successful in doing so is not about special genes or special brains but is instead a matter of how well we leverage our brain's ability to change, through practice.

It's worth mentioning that, for years, scientists who studied the brain did not think the adult brain was plastic. Well into the twentieth century, neuroscience dogma held that brains could not change after development. "You can't teach old brains new tricks," said the neuroscientists.

This message, coupled with the discovery of DNA, undoubtedly contributed to the idea that we humans, and our brains, were fixed and immutable entities. Understanding this scientific history provided a window into the roots of this bizarre delusion, and its staying power.

I now play multiple musical instruments and learned them almost entirely as an adult. At present, my parents are in their seventies, and neither plays an instrument.

My daughter is a phenomenal artist. She's been drawing since she could hold a crayon. Her drawing abilities surpassed my own and those of my wife when she was around seven or eight years old.

How do these things square with the innate talent narrative? Are we to believe it is all the work of some fortuitous genetic mutation? The principle of parsimony would beg to differ.

Fortunately, change is in the air. Attitudes in this area have shifted significantly since my childhood days. They've even shifted significantly since I first began writing about these topics a decade or so ago. Several voices have helped spark this much-needed shift.

Thanks in large part to the work of Carol Dweck, people now widely embrace the concept of the "growth mindset," or the idea that abilities are not inborn but developed through practice and effort.

Malcolm Gladwell has popularized the "10,000-hour rule," which says that when it comes to developing expertise, practice is the differentiator.

Tim Ferriss has demonstrated how, by being thoughtful about how we practice, we can develop expertise in a fraction of the amount of time once thought possible.

And Daniel Coyle's study of the world's "talent factories" has convincingly shown that "greatness is not born, it's grown."

But we're still in the early days. We've only just begun to explore this terrain, and to combine theoretical insights acquired through studying the mechanisms of neuroplasticity with the empirical knowledge gleaned from studying world-class learners.

Furthermore, the residue of our mass delusion remains. The notion that some people are born musical, or artistic, or athletic is still widely held. Even those who profess to embrace the growth mindset may often only apply it selectively.

Which means there's plenty more work to be done in eradicating the talent myth. For me, the seed that was planted all those years ago ultimately grew into what is now Brainjo. The initial mission of Brainjo was to bring these concepts into the realm of music. That's the subject of the book you're now holding.

But, for me, it's ultimately about more than learning music. I believe that, based on what we've learned about the brain in recent decades, most people are capable of far more than they realize. But realizing that remarkable potential first requires shedding the beliefs that constrain it.

It first requires believing in that potential.

I know that the talent myth has discouraged countless people from ever pursuing their musical ambitions. Giving people both the confidence and the tools needed to do so has been immensely rewarding. And the benefits usually go well beyond music making. Once a mind is released from the grip of the talent myth, a whole new world of possibility opens up.

I hope that this book not only helps you realize your own musical ambitions but also opens up that new world to you. In gratitude,

Josh Turknett, MD

ANYONE CAN PLAY MUSIC

ABOUT THIS BOOK

. . . .

WHO'S THIS FOR?

This book is a compilation of key principles, concepts, and techniques related to learning a musical instrument (though applicable to learning any complex skill). As such, you should find each chapter to be self-contained and fully digestible on its own. While the order in which you read them isn't critical, you will likely benefit most from reading through them sequentially your first time through. After that point, feel free to peruse them in as random and haphazard a fashion as you please.

As a result of this organization, you will find certain concepts and principles repeated. Since repetition is key to retention, I invite you to view this as a feature rather than a bug.

You will also find that when examples require an instrument-specific context, the banjo is usually chosen to fill that role. This is because, while I play a few instruments, I consider myself a banjo player first and foremost. But rest assured that these principles will apply to any music-making device!

WHY BRAINJO?

. . . .

Brains and banjos. To most, they are an unlikely pair. But for me, they've been the twin obsessions of my life.

My obsession with the brain first took hold with an eighth-grade science project and then blossomed in college, where I earned a degree in cognitive neuroscience. After concluding I'd learn more about the brain in the clinic than the laboratory, I pursued medical school and residency training in neurology. My interest in the brain has always revolved around cognition, including an enduring fascination with the mechanisms and applications of the science of learning and neuroplasticity.

My obsession with the banjo began on Christmas Day 2001. My first banjo was a gift from my family. I'd actually fallen in love with the instrument long before that when, at the age of three, I first heard Kermit the Frog pluck the iconic opening lick of "The Rainbow Connection."

I'll admit that the prospect of learning to play was overwhelming and intimidating at first. I could scarcely fathom how I could ever make music like the expert pickers I loved.

And, according to conventional wisdom, the odds were not in my favor. First, nobody in my family played. Second, I hadn't started playing as a kid. And third, I didn't have several hours a day to devote to practicing. On the contrary, I was smack-dab in the middle of a medical internship, which meant working upward of ninety grueling hours a week.

Nonetheless, I was determined to give it my best. Plus, music provided a much-needed sanctuary from the demands of medical training. Even just strumming the open strings of the banjo would reliably brighten my day.

It was during this time that I had a revelation: What if I could utilize my understanding of neuroplasticity to augment my learning process? Could I realize my banjo dreams by practicing smarter and not harder?

So, that's what I did. And it worked. Remarkably well.

I progressed much faster than I thought I would. Faster than I'd been told I would, especially given my limited practice time, which seldom amounted to more than ten to twenty minutes a day. In a few months, I was making music that I'd previously thought was out of reach for me.

That experience left me with a nagging question: Why wasn't this common practice? Why wasn't anyone in the world of music education, or just education in general, talking about neuroplasticity?

We knew that, in order to learn anything, whether it's how to tie our shoes, make an omelet, conjugate a verb, or solve a differential equation, our brain must change. And yet, the science of brain change was glaringly absent from our approach to education.

We'd learned so much about how brains changed, yet almost no one was reaping the benefits. And I knew firsthand how powerful it could be.

Even worse, much of what we learned had shown that many of

our common learning practices were either ineffective or downright detrimental. This was certainly true when it came to common approaches to learning music. Neuroscience had revealed that human potential was so much greater than we'd thought, but almost all of it was still going unrealized.

It was this experience that sparked the idea for what would later become Brainjo. I knew that one day I not only wanted to spread this knowledge but integrate it into a formal system of instruction.

It took more than a decade to turn that vision into a reality, when the first courses of musical instruction at the Brainjo Academy were released. The goal of the courses is to provide the most efficient and effective path to learning music so that anyone, at any age, can play.

Since that time, thousands of people have done just that, many of whom had no prior musical background, and many of whom had previously thought music making wasn't in the cards for them. They've been able to experience the same transformative benefits that I have.

The courses at the academy are based on the Brainjo Method, the system of instruction I'd envisioned years ago that would incorporate the core principles of learning and neuroplasticity. This book is about those principles, referred to as the "Laws of Brainjo."

The gift of neuroplasticity means that we can mold our minds to acquire new complex knowledge and skills, like learning a musical instrument, at any age. Every skill we humans possess is learned. And it is how we learn, and how we practice, that trigger the brain change that makes this possible.

That means that failures in learning are not failures of aptitude but failures of process. Mastering brain change is how we release the spectacular potential in every brain. What could be more important?

Note: if you'd like to learn more about Brainjo and the courses of instruction based on the Brainjo Method, head over to brainjo. academy.

1

THE FIRST LAW

· ·

Ten thousand hours.

You may be familiar with this figure.

Based on research by Anders Ericsson and popularized in Malcolm Gladwell's book *Outliers,* it's the average number of hours across disciplines that research shows it takes to become an expert. The average amount of time it takes to master something.

The take-home message from the 10,000-hour rule is that, despite the stories we share as part of our cultural mythology, passion and dedication are the key determinants of mastery. From sculpting to picking, humans get really, really good at stuff through hard work, not through some fortuitous genetic gift of talent.

Now, you can read this two ways.

On the one hand, this is a very *encouraging* notion, as it means that when it comes to your musical goals, virtually anything is possible. With consistent, focused effort, the sky is the limit.

On the other hand, ten thousand hours is nothing to sneeze at. If you can manage two hours of practice every day, then you'll reach your musical Shangri-La in roughly thirteen years, eight months. To someone strumming their first guitar chords, blowing their first B-flat on the tuba, or plucking their first note on the 5-string banjo, those kind of numbers might be a little *discouraging*.

But there's more to this story. Specifically, there are a few very important points that are usually overlooked in the ten-thousand-hours conversation.

1. Even more important than how much we practice is **how we practice.**

Ten thousand hours are an *average*. If we were to take all the data points and plot them out, we'd get a bell-shaped distribution, with the apex of our bell at the ten-thousand-hours mark. Something like this:

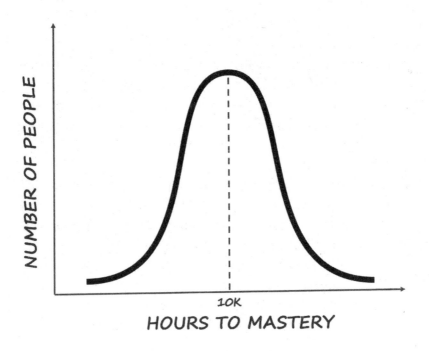

So some people in this data set have spent a good bit more than ten thousand hours to achieve mastery.

And some have spent a good bit less.

So, what explains this difference? Why do some people take much longer to achieve the same results? And why do some people never reach mastery at all?

It's better genes, of course! Nothing but good ol'-fashioned "natural talent," right?

Wrong! The difference maker is *how* they practiced.

The rate-limiting factor here, the primary constraint on the learning process, is the pace at which the brain changes. And that pace is largely defined by our biology—in other words, in properties of our nervous system that are common to all of us. Those who reached mastery faster were simply better at changing their brains. They practiced more effectively, in a manner that fully capitalized on the biological mechanisms that support learning.

2. Most people give up.

Most people who set about to master anything, musical instruments included, ultimately end up giving up. There are surely more guitars collecting dust in closets and attics than there are ones being picked lovingly every day by skilled players.

And why do the majority give up? If mastery is just about putting in the hours, is it just because they're lazy?

No.

They don't give up because of a character flaw. They give up because they stop getting better. Research tells us that the single greatest motivator for learning is progress. Progress is the reward that keeps us coming back for more. On the flip side, nobody plods on for long in the face of no progress.

And what causes people to stop progressing? Ineffective practice.

In this age of information, we are blessed with an abundance of learning materials. It's simple to find *what* we should be learning.

But *how* we should go about learning that material is seldom, if ever, addressed specifically. In spite of the fact that it's the single biggest determinant of success or failure, how to practice is rarely considered or communicated.

That needs to change.

3. The greatest proportion of improvements occurs early in the learning process.

This concept, which applies to all sorts of various phenomena, is often referred to as the "80/20 rule" (or the "Pareto Principle," after the economist who first suggested it).

In this instance, the 80/20 rule states that 80 percent of your results are achieved through 20 percent of your efforts. In other words, provided that we're mindful of our learning process, and that we correctly identify what that 20 percent is, we can achieve most of our gains in those first two thousand hours. After that, we start facing diminishing returns on our time investment. The final stages of mastery, which take up a disproportionate amount of time, are about putting in long hours for gains that are often imperceptible to the casual observer.

If we plot this concept out graphically, it looks like this:

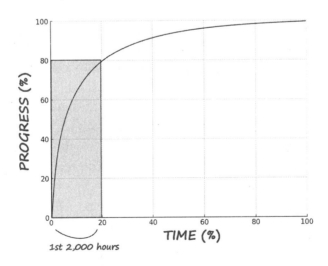

Again, this is a very encouraging notion. But, once again, it also highlights just how important it is for us to be mindful of how we learn and practice, and what we stand to gain if we are.

THE FIRST LAW OF BRAINJO

Without a doubt, mastering any skill, including a musical instrument, requires focused, consistent effort. That said, ten thousand hours of any-old practice won't magically get us where we want to go. Masters don't become masters through the sheer force of will alone. It's a necessary but not sufficient condition.

Masters become masters because somehow—be it luck, a great mentor, or natural disposition—they've managed to unlock the right process for learning. A process that leads to consistent, rewarding progress.

Replicate this process, and you too can enjoy similar results. Which brings us to the **First Law of Brainjo:**

To learn to
play like the masters,
you must
learn to play
like the masters.

Unlocking the secrets of and maximizing the brain's capacity for growth and change have been intense personal and professional areas interest of mine for two decades now.

In this book, we will continue to extract insights from the fields of learning, mastery, and neuroplasticity to build a set of maxims for effective practice, and, in so doing, create a road map for helping us to mold a musical mind.

2

FLUENCY OR RECITATION?

. . . .

"Let's play a tune together. I'll back you up."

"Sounds great!" I replied, trying my best to project confidence as my stomach contents migrated their way up my esophagus.

It was my first banjo camp. Banjo camps are immersive experiences where banjo enthusiasts take workshops from and play music with expert players. It's all banjo, all the time. One person's heaven is another's hell, I know.

At the time I'd been learning bluegrass banjo for a little more than a year, and one of my favorite players—a bona fide banjo Jedi with decades of experience—had just asked *me* to jam with him. I couldn't refuse.

"What do you want to play?" he asked.

I mentally searched my small repertoire of tunes, looking for one I thought I could nail. I wanted to showcase just how far I'd come in such a short time.

"'Fireball Mail'?" I suggested.

"Great. I'll kick it off."

Here goes nothing, I thought.

He played a few pickup notes, and, with a mixture of excitement and terror, I launched into my banjo solo. A solo I'd probably played at home somewhere north of thirty-five thousand times.

It didn't take long for me to realize things were not going well. For starters, my timing was *awful!* For the life of me, I couldn't get my playing to sync up with his. Was he the problem? Was he just not good at keeping time?

Uh, not likely.

Things only got worse. I was playing all the wrong notes, and it seemed that all the right ones had vanished from my fretboard. It felt like the first time I'd held a banjo. Cleanly picking a banjo string seemed about as easy as hitting a bull's-eye from eight miles away in a blizzard.

Anxiety rapidly morphed into blind panic. Beads of sweat from my forehead began trickling down my brow, searing my eyeballs. My heart was thudding in my ears. *Just breathe,* I tried telling myself. If only I could remember how!

Finally, I just stopped playing, putting both of us out of our misery. "I'm sorry," I said, "I guess I need to practice that one a little more." He nodded in agreement, with a look of pity that made me want to vanish into thin air.

"Just keep at it. You'll get there," he replied mercifully.

Yes, I was humiliated. But I was also *baffled* by what had just transpired. I'd played this tune flawlessly time and again at home. I thought it was one of my best. Had all those many hours of practice been for nothing?

It seemed that something more than nerves had sabotaged my performance, and I was determined to figure out what. Because I *never* wanted that to happen again. I vowed then that next time would be different. What I didn't realize at the time was that honoring that vow would require going back to the beginning.

THE TWO ROUTES TO MUSIC MAKING

There are two main ways humans make music. Understanding this difference, and understanding which way of making music you want to learn, is essential knowledge for every aspiring musician.

The fundamental difference between these two ways boils down to where the music *originates* in the music-making process. In the first way, music originates from symbols printed on a page of sheet music. Technically, the ultimate source of the music is the composer who translated the music in their mind into symbols on paper.

The symbols on the paper tell the musician what notes to play, when to play them, and for how long. Musicians who play this way spend much of their practice time learning how to decode these symbols, a process referred to as "sight-reading." Sight-reading musicians function as a conduit between the mind of the composer and the listener. Like a cook following a recipe, they carry out the composer's instructions as accurately as possible in order to faithfully reproduce the music from the composer's imagination.

To acquire the ability to play music from notation, a sight-reading musician must create networks in the visual cortex that interpret written symbols and then transform those instructions into the corresponding movement patterns. While modifications to those movements are made based on auditory feedback, the eyes are the ones running the show, since visual information is being translated into music.

In the second way of making music, often referred to as playing "by ear," the music originates in the mind of the performer. The performer spends much of their practice time learning how to match the sounds of their instrument to the sounds they imagine. Ultimately, a musician who plays by ear builds connections that map musical thoughts in the auditory cortex onto movement patterns for the limbs, enabling their imagined sounds to come out of their instrument.

If we consider the analogs of these skills in the realm of language, learning to play by notation is like learning how to read aloud. Developing the skill of reading aloud requires building neural networks that can translate written words into speech. As with musical notation, the thoughts that are conveyed originate not in the reader's own mind but in the imagination of the writer. We can refer to this as the skill of "recitation."

On the other hand, learning to play music by ear is like learning how to communicate via spoken language. Developing this skill requires that we build neural networks that can translate our own thoughts into speech. This is how we all learned to talk, and we commonly refer to this skill as "fluency." Fluency is what allows us to have conversations, where ideas are transmitted from one mind to another.

Now, consider a scenario where you're moving to Brazil and need to be able to communicate with the people there. Which of these skills would you need to learn? Fluency, of course. The ability to read Portuguese writing aloud, or the ability to recite Portuguese, would be inadequate for your purposes. This is obvious, and I doubt anyone would make the mistake of learning the skill of recitation when fluency was what they needed. And yet, this sort of mistake is common when it comes to learning music.

THE MASTER'S PATH

When it comes to bluegrass banjo, Earl Scruggs is the standard-bearer. His syncopated, staccato picking is considered the defining sound of bluegrass music. For many, learning to play bluegrass banjo is synonymous with learning to play like Earl.

Earl's banjo playing first took the world by storm in 1945 when he was hired by Bill Monroe to be part of his band, Bill Monroe & The Bluegrass Boys. Earl's innovative licks and picking patterns were inscrutable to many, including aspiring banjoists who wanted to emulate his playing. In fact, Earl's style was even inscrutable to himself (more on this in another chapter).

Finally, in 1968, the Rosetta stone of Scruggs was published, in the form of a book titled *Earl Scruggs and the 5-String Banjo*. The book contained banjo tablatures (a form of written notation for stringed instruments) for many of Earl's most iconic solos. For many aspiring players, especially those with limited access to a community of bluegrass musicians, this book became their primary source for learning to play Scruggs-style banjo. And, more generally, learning bluegrass banjo using tabs as the primary source material became a common way in which it was learned and taught.

However, there's one problem: Earl Scruggs never used tabs or any kind of musical notation. As mentioned, Earl couldn't even describe to people how he played. It was banjo player Bill Keith, not Earl, who transcribed Earl's playing into tabs.

As is the case with virtually every folk tradition, bluegrass musicians play by ear, not by sight-reading. Playing bluegrass music requires developing the skill of fluency. When I sat down to pick a tune with one of my banjo heroes that fateful day at banjo camp, he was trying to have a musical conversation. Yet I, like so many other frustrated banjoists, had inadvertently learned the skill of recitation instead. As a result, we couldn't communicate.

Though I didn't realize it at the time, I had violated the First Law of Brainjo: to learn to play like the masters, we must *learn to play* like the masters. Like so many others, I'd set about to learn how to play like Earl Scruggs but followed an entirely different learning path than he had! My failure that day had nothing to do with lacking talent and everything to do with developing the wrong skill. I'd simply followed the wrong learning path.

BRAINJO LAW #2: When charting your musical journey, make sure you first know your destination.

Unfortunately, this story has unfolded for thousands of banjo players over the years, responsible for countless dashed dreams and neglected banjos. It has given bluegrass banjo the undeserved reputation of being especially hard, which easily can and often does become a self-fulfilling prophecy. However, this hasn't just become the typical story of aspiring bluegrass banjo players; it's become the typical story for anyone trying to learn to play music in any genre that requires fluency.

So, why does this happen so often? Why is it still the norm for people who want to learn the skill of fluency to end up learning the skill of recitation instead? Much of it can be traced to the stories we currently tell about innate abilities and musical potential.

THE TALKING "NATURALS"

Imagine a world where, starting tomorrow, it becomes illegal to talk to children. Any communication with people under the age of eighteen must be nonverbal. Once children enter school, they are permitted to learn to read aloud, if they choose to do so. The only time speaking is allowed in this world is when reading text out loud.

However, a few small towns, villages, and a handful of rebel families defy these rules. These outlaws continue to talk to their children as they've always done, unlike the rest of the world.

In this world, what would happen to language?

Most people would become mute, and conversations would cease. The "reciters," those who elected to learn how to read aloud in school, could read texts written by people long ago, even if no one could understand the meaning of their words.

The rarest breed of all would be the "talkers"—individuals with the seemingly magical ability to conjure words from nowhere, without relying on written text. The rest of the world would marvel at their gifts, insisting that they must have been born with their abilities, since they clearly had not learned them in school.

As absurd as this story sounds, this appears to have been precisely what has happened in recent history with our relationship to music. Humans have been making music for tens of thousands of years. For most of that time, it was something we all did. We didn't divide ourselves into the performers and the listeners, the professionals and the amateurs. Just as we all learn to talk now, we all learned to make music then. We developed the skill of fluency in our native music back then in the same way we develop the skill of fluency in our native language now.

At some point, we stopped developing musical fluency naturally. And we started developing a new way of making music that involved reading symbols on a piece of paper, primarily to serve the needs of what we now know as classical music. People who wanted to play this kind of music had to be taught how to decipher those symbols, and so a formal system of instruction emerged.

Eventually, for many, learning to play music became synonymous with learning to sight-read. Not because it's the natural or superior way to make music but as an artifact of history.

However, in some parts of the world and in some families, those ancient traditions didn't stop. In these places, children still grow up becoming fluent in both language and music. Just like the "talkers" in our story, those folks are commonly viewed as possessing some special, innate gift.

You've likely heard or read people marveling at the fact that some great musician "can't even read music!" Again, this is because we often think learning to play music means learning to sight-read. Yet, the overwhelming majority of great musicians in the course of human history couldn't read music! Because the overwhelming majority of musicians in the course of human history, including the musicians of today, don't play music by sight-reading.

The reality, which should be abundantly clear by now, is that playing music using our eyes is much more counterintuitive and peculiar than using our ears! As a species, we've been learning music with our ears much longer than we've been learning with our eyes, which of course makes perfect sense. Twenty thousand years ago, I doubt anyone would've predicted that humans would one day make music by looking at squiggles on a piece of paper!

Our attitudes and beliefs about music have led to the strange new world of today. Understanding how and why it's so odd matters for two main reasons.

First, many people don't believe they can learn to play with their ears. We've come to think, for the reasons mentioned above, that this is an innate gift. It is not. It is learned, just like every other cognitive skill you have.

Second, people who want to develop the skill of fluency often end up developing the skill of recitation instead. This happens partly because of the misconception that learning music equates to learning to sight-read, and partly due to a lack of resources for helping people develop the skill of fluency. Following the wrong path inevitably leads to frustration and disappointment, and all too often, the abandonment of musical hopes and dreams because of the false impression they didn't have what it takes.

CHARTING YOUR COURSE: FLUENCY OR RECITATION?

Much of this book is about how to learn, or how to apply the science of neuroplasticity to make your learning more efficient and effective. These principles apply regardless of whether you're developing the skill of fluency or recitation. Learning any complex skill is a journey, with many steps along the way. Understanding how we learn helps us reliably progress from one step to the next, bringing us ever closer to our destination.

However, before we spend weeks, months, or years taking those steps, it makes sense to take a moment to ensure that we've charted our course for the right destination! So, before we dive into the nitty-gritty details of how to change our brains, let's be certain that we're clear about the kind of change we need.

How do you know if you need to develop fluency or recitation? For the most part, it depends on the kind of music you want to make. As a simple rule, if the musicians who play your chosen instrument in your chosen genre play with sheet music in front of them, you need recitation. If they don't, you need fluency. The following chart summarizes the skill typically required by the major genres of music:

Genres Requiring Fluency (aurally-based)	Genres Requiring Recitation (notation-based)
Rock and Roll	Classical
Pop	Big Band Jazz
Blues	Opera
Country	
Reggae	
Folk (contemporary and traditional)	
Bluegrass	
Hip-Hop	
Jazz (small group and solo)	

3

THE ADVANTAGES
OF AN ADULT BRAIN

. . . .

I'm older and have never played an instrument. Can I still learn?

This question, or some variation of it, is one I receive quite often. Buried inside it are a whole range of assumptions. Assumptions about childhood, about inborn talents and abilities, and about the ability of older brains to learn new things.

Thanks to advances in neuroscience over the last several decades, there is now no denying that we all possess a brain capable of changing itself throughout our life. And since changing the brain is the biological foundation of all learning, we can learn to play any new skill, including playing an instrument, whether we're eight or eighty.

Be that as it may, there are some who may still believe that starting out "later in life" is a disadvantage.

But I'd argue just the opposite.

I'd argue that, while there may be certain advantages to learning during childhood, the scales tilt in favor of the older brain. Here's why:

FOUR ADVANTAGES OF HAVING AN ADULT BRAIN

Adult Advantage #1: FOCUS

Focused, undivided attention is essential to learning. It would be wasteful for us to remember everything in the course of our daily life, and it's only when we pay close attention to something that our brain tags it for further encoding and storage while we sleep.

Attention, then, is the gatekeeper of neuroplasticity. In other words, sustained, single-minded focus is required for our brain to change itself in response to practice.

When we pay close attention to something, widely connected neurons toward the base of the frontal lobe bathe their targets in the neurotransmitter acetylcholine. It's the chemical cue that says "this is important."

In childhood, those circuits mediating attention and concentration haven't fully matured. Anyone who's spent time around a nine-year-old boy can attest that sustaining focus isn't typically his strong suit. And these circuits don't fully mature until we're in our early 20's.

Adult Advantage #2: DELIBERATE PRACTICE

As covered in chapter 1, *how* we practice matters far more than *how much* we practice. Those outliers who reach mastery several times faster don't do so by dint of DNA, but because they practice strategically. They focus relentlessly on areas of weakness until they become areas of strength. And they don't waste time practicing what they've already learned well. This process is sometimes referred to as "deliberate practice."

Deliberate practice not only requires careful planning but an honest appraisal of one's abilities—and honest self-assessment is also something that improves with age. As the years and life's hard knocks accumulate, ego declines, and humility rises. Our finely honed inner critic can be an asset, *provided we put it to good use.*

Adult Advantage #3: MOTIVATION

Let's face it, most kids taking music lessons don't actually want to be there. I imagine we could end world hunger if we could recover all the money wasted on piano, guitar, and violin instruction during childhood.

Learning can't be forced. It just isn't going to happen without the desire to learn. You can't manufacture intrinsic motivation.

But this isn't a problem for the adult learner. If you've decided to tackle a musical instrument later in life, you're doing so because it's something you really want.

Those childhood "prodigies" that show up in your Facebook feed playing *Foggy Mountain Banjo* at blistering speed capture your attention precisely because they are extraordinary. They're the exceptions that prove the rule.

Adult Advantage #4: TIME

I'm specifically talking about those of you who've decided to take the banjo plunge in your golden years, after you've shed many of the responsibilities of work and family and are now free to pursue passions you've kept on the back burner.

You have the time to not only practice but to do all those other things that feed your banjo-learning brain, like listening to copious amounts of great music, studying those musicians you love most, and getting out and playing music with your peers.

STEALING FROM CHILDREN

Now, don't get me wrong. The deck isn't stacked entirely in the favor of those with well-aged neurons. Things do slow down a bit inside the brain with age, at least in most.

Thanks to things like advanced-glycation end products and oxidative damage, the speed of a typical human's nerve impulses declines by about 3% every 10 years. That's not huge, but it's enough to matter.

Even that decline is not an inevitable product of aging, however, and something that can likely be modified considerably through diet and lifestyle (the precise details of which are beyond the scope of this discussion). Furthermore, the magnitude of slowing also isn't enough to matter when it comes to the demands of music making.

I saw Doc Watson playing live well into his eighties. Even though I imagine he could've played at a faster clip fifty years prior, not once did I think, *Sounds great, if only it were faster.*

Sure, losing those lightning-fast neuronal transmission speeds of youth means you probably won't be setting the world record for speed picking in your sixties, but it's a happy coincidence that, by the time you've reached that age, you've long ago stopped caring about such things.

The other area where the kids have the advantage, and where we bigger folks should take note, is that kids aren't afraid of screwing up. As we get older, though, we tend to become increasingly intolerant of making mistakes. We get used to feeling competent and skilled in most areas of life, which leads us to avoid doing things that make us feel incompetent and unskilled. So we stop trying to learn hard things.

Why is the willingness to screw up so important? Because it's how we learn. In fact, it's the *only* way we learn.

Remember: in order to improve, in order to get better at anything, our brain must change. This, of course, is why understanding the science of brain change can help us become much more effective at learning.

And the reason our brain changes is so that it can do something that it can't already do. Your brain still can't quite get your fingers to form that D chord in time, for example, so you make a mistake. That mistake is what triggers your brain to rewire itself until one day, you can do it.

If we don't make any mistakes, our brain has no reason to change! Mistakes are how we get better because mistakes are how we trigger the brain to change. All the master musicians we revere got really, really good by relentlessly screwing up!

But maintaining that youthful willingness to make mistakes may do more than bring you closer to your musical goal, it may literally make your brain younger. How so?

THINKING YOUNGER

When I began my neurology training at the turn of the twenty-first century, there was tremendous hope and optimism around the prospect of finding a drug cure for Alzheimer's disease (AD). And for good reason. The 1990s had been the decade of the brain. A huge investment of resources had been made in brain research, much of which had been directed toward investigating the neuropathology of AD. As a result, we'd learned a lot. Many experts in the field thought we were on the cusp of translating that knowledge into a major pharmaceutical breakthrough.

So did I. And I wanted to be a part of it.

Early in my career as a neurologist, I worked for a leading clinical research center. That included my involvement in multiple clinical trials for AD to find that breakthrough.

But the breakthrough never came. As each passing year brought one disappointing result after another, our collective hope and optimism turned into doubt and frustration. I no longer believe that a drug cure is in our future.

The situation is far from hopeless, however. In fact, there's more reason for optimism than ever before.

The search for a drug was motivated by the belief that AD was caused by something like a bad gene or a defective protein. A nefarious molecule that you could target and eradicate with a drug.

What we've learned instead is that age-related cognitive decline and the most common form of AD are driven by lifestyle, resulting from the combined impact of a great many factors. That's not the sort of thing that can be cured with a drug.

And do you know what factor many researchers now believe to be the most impactful of all? Cognitive activity. That's because those who lead the most cognitively demanding lives are much less likely to suffer from cognitive decline and dementia.

Put another way, those who stimulate the most brain change over the course of their lives maintain the healthiest, youngest looking brains.

You've probably seen the difference between the body of a seventy-five-year-old who's been working out in the gym all his life and one who hasn't exercised since his teens. The body of an older man who has continued to challenge it regularly not only looks healthier, but it is also much more *capable*. While harder to appreciate because they're hidden from view, our brains are the same. The more we challenge them, the healthier they look and the more capable they become.

In our youth, our brain is always changing. In the first couple of decades of our life, we must acquire all the cognitive skills we need to become independent, fully functioning adults. That requires ongoing plastic reorganization across the entire brain. And a large body of research indicates that this ongoing stimulation of plastic change is what keeps the brain in pristine condition. When we challenge our brain, it sends a signal that we need to keep it in tip-top condition.

For the typical adult today, the cognitive demands of life drop considerably by middle age. By this time in our lives, we can spend most of our time in "autopilot" mode if we wish, reaping the fruits of our brain-changing labor. In early life, triggering continuous brain change is a necessity. After that, it is a choice. Our brain doesn't stop changing because it can't, it stops because we no longer ask it to.

If the drop in whole-brain stimulation that comes from learning complex skills drives the deterioration of our brain, then what's the remedy? Never stop learning hard things.

And what do many experts, me included, consider to be an ideal activity for whole-brain stimulation? Learning a musical instrument.

Yet, the only way we actually reap music's ability to restore youth is if we trigger brain change. And what again must we do to trigger brain change? Make mistakes!

From this perspective, we shouldn't lament our mistakes, we should celebrate them. Mistakes provide priceless, brain-saving stimulation that will help us continue doing the things we love most for as long as possible. How poetic it is that not being afraid of mistakes, like a child, is the key to keeping our brain young.

4

HOW TO PLAY "IN THE ZONE," AND WHY YOU WANT TO BE THERE

. . . .

"I was playing out of my head."

"It was like the banjo was playing itself."

"I was in the zone."

Ask a master—regardless of domain—what it feels like when they're performing at their very best, and these are the kind of descriptions you're apt to hear. The words may be different, but the underlying sentiment is almost always the same: an alternate state of consciousness has been reached, allowing for effortless and optimal performance.

Over the years, different names have been used to describe this state of being: "the zone," "flow state," "Zen-like." In these moments, the conscious mind is quiet, sometimes leaving the player with the impression that he or she is no longer involved in the playing, perhaps even feeling a bit sheepish about taking credit for the resultant performance.

But the zone isn't territory reserved just for masters. On the contrary, these moments of effortless execution can happen to anyone, at any stage in the learning process. In fact, you'd be wise to make it a habit of seeking them out often, just as the masters do. Here's why.

THE BIRD'S-EYE VIEW OF LEARNING

Nobody is born knowing how to play music. This is obvious. Even Jimi Hendrix had to build his own guitar-playing brain.

This means that every component of playing music, from picking a string or fretting a note on the guitar, to forming chord shapes on the piano, must be learned.

More specifically, it means that a dedicated neural network—a set of instructions for how to perform that particular skill, written in the language of neurons—needs to be created for each and every technical component of playing.

The brilliant thing about the human brain is that it can create those instructions for itself, based entirely on the inputs it's given through practice (which in reality are the inputs it provides itself . . . consider your mind blown).

In chess and Tai Chi master Josh Waitzkin's book *The Art of Learning,* he likens the learning process to hacking a path through dense jungle with a machete. At first the task is arduous and taxing, with great expense of time and effort.

During this stage, the conscious mind is fully engaged, frantically trying to cobble together an ad hoc motor program (i.e., a set of instructions for movement) out of existing multipurpose neural machinery. All cognitive resources are brought to bear on the task at hand.

If we place a subject at this stage of learning in a functional brain imaging scanner, we see widespread increases in brain activity.

With repeated practice over time, things change. A lot.

Ultimately, if the learning process goes well, the brain creates a customized neural network for the learned activity. When the task is performed now, we see both a shift in the location and overall amount of brain activation.

This neural network that's been created not only consumes fewer resources, but much of it also now exists in brain areas "beneath" the cortex. In technical jargon, it is largely "subcortical."

After learning, we get more with less. And that knowledge, which consists of the motor program for executing that skill, is literally now a part of you. Or, more specifically, a part of your brain.

Thinking back to our jungle analogy, a path has now been cleared, allowing us to walk down it effortlessly, without any contribution from the conscious mind. Through practice, a new pathway has literally been carved in the brain.

THE PURPOSE OF PRACTICE

So, what might this have to do with playing "in the zone"?

Everything.

Playing "in the zone" can only happen after these paths have been cleared, after we've built neural networks specific to the corresponding activity through effective practice.

The truth is, you enter the zone all the time, every day. Walking down the street, brushing your teeth, driving a car, fixing a sandwich—these are all learned skills you can perform while your conscious mind is engaged in something else (we take these activities, complicated as they are, for granted, precisely because they feel so effortless). Each of these activities has its own pathway carved in the brain, a dedicated neural network containing its set of instructions, built and reinforced through years of practice.

Creating these neural pathways is the reason we practice. Which brings us to the **Third Law of Brainjo:**

BRAINJO LAW #3: The primary purpose of practice is to provide your brain the data it needs to build a neural network.

The goal of practice is not to get better right then and there. The goal is to signal the brain that we want it to change and provide it with the inputs it needs to do so effectively.

But this raises a critical point. If our brain is building new networks based on the inputs we provide, then we need to ensure that we're providing it with the right *kinds* of inputs, at the right *time*. The brain will build a network, a set of task-specific instructions, based on any type of repeated input that it cares about. Provide the wrong kind of input, and we end up with the wrong kind of network.

Practice picking your guitar sloppily over and over again, and guess what you'll end up with? A sloppy-guitar-picking neural network. Like it or not, that network is now yours forever. In other words, when we carve new pathways in the brain, it pays to ensure they end up leading us where we want to go.

KNOWING WHEN (AND WHEN NOT) TO MOVE ON

In the beginning, the temptation is always to go too fast. We're excited and eager to start playing great music, and we want to play it now!

But the danger here in giving in to the urge to go quickly is that you move to more advanced techniques before the basic ones they're grounded in have fully developed. You move on before those foundational pathways have been laid.

Rinse and repeat this process, and you end up with a web of networks that don't do what you want them to do. A house of cards that places a hard ceiling on your future potential, and the only remedy for which is to start over, building a new and improved web of networks (much easier said than done!).

But what if there was a way we could know when those pathways were fully formed, a way to know when it was safe for us to move onward to the next hurdle? As it turns out, there is.

In neuroscience terms, when a skill no longer requires our conscious mind for its execution, it is said to have become "automatic." This can be tested for experimentally by having a subject perform the skill in question while their attention is diverted elsewhere. If there's no decline in performance, then the skill meets the criteria for "automaticity." If performance declines, then more practice is needed.

So, if we want to test for automaticity ourselves, we can steal this same strategy, which brings us to our next law:

BRAINJO LAW #4: Work on one new foundational skill at a time until it becomes automatic.

Now, I know what you're probably thinking: *How do I know if a skill has become automatic?*

Experimentally, in snazzy neuroscience studies, automaticity is usually tested by having a subject perform the learned skill while engaging in some arbitrary task on a computer—counting the number of blue squares that flash by, for example.

But is there a way for us to test automaticity for ourselves without any kind of specially designed digital equipment? Might there be some kind of device that's tailor-made for the business of banjo learning, inexpensive, and delightfully analog?

Why of course. Here it is:

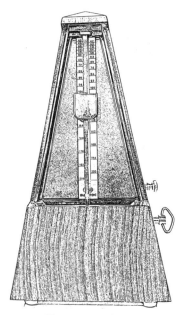

The Metronome

Now, before you run away screaming, let me explain.

I know the metronome has a dicey reputation. Like eating liver, flossing nightly, or routine colonoscopies, it's one of those things you know is probably good for you but you don't exactly enjoy doing. So, you put it off or avoid it altogether.

If so, it's time we changed your relationship to the metronome, because as you'll soon discover it's an indispensable tool in your learning arsenal, and using it can actually be great fun.

In my view, the metronome's largely undeserved reputation is mainly based on two things.

First, playing along with the metronome isn't something that comes naturally. For most folks, it's not entirely clear what you're supposed to be doing amid all the incessant clicking. Do you only play with the clicks? In between the clicks? And what the heck is "largo" and "allegro," anyhow?

So, just like you must know how a melody goes before you set about to play it, you must know how whatever you're playing is supposed to sound along with the metronome before you get started. Otherwise, you've sabotaged yourself from the start.

Second, and most relevant to this discussion, is that folks tend to misinterpret the feedback they get from the metronome. Especially if it isn't positive.

You see, most people think of the metronome as a tool for practicing their timing. And yes, it's useful for this. But a greater—and often neglected—purpose of the metronome is as a test for automaticity.

Consider: in order for you to successfully play along and in sync with the metronome, you must listen closely to its clicking while simultaneously making the proper movements of your picking and fretting hand to produce the desired sounds from your instrument.

Thus, when playing with the metronome, you're performing a learned skill (whatever it is you're practicing on your instrument that day) while your conscious mind is focused on something else (the metronome). And, to do this successfully, you must perform the learned skill just as well as you would without the metronome clicking away. In other words, the learned skill (your playing) mustn't degrade even when your attention is directed elsewhere.

This, my friends, is *priceless* feedback. Here we have a simple, inexpensive tool capable of peering into the brain and assessing the state of our developing neural networks. The perfect test for automaticity.

Unfortunately, this is not how most people seem to interpret metronome feedback. The most common conclusion when things don't go so well is "I guess I'm just no good with playing with the metronome" or, worse yet, "I'm a lousy player."

But both of those conclusions are unjustified. And they stem from a basic misconception of what the metronome is all about, and why it's useful.

So, here's a better, more productive, way to think about it. If you try playing along with the metronome and it doesn't go so well, all it means is that the skill has yet to become automatic. If you must devote your attention to the movement of your hands when the metronome is clicking, then it is *biologically impossible* to play in sync with it. The path just isn't fully formed, and so a little more time is needed in the woodshed. We are all bound by the laws of neurobiology.

I should point out here, though it may be obvious to you, that you can use things besides a metronome for this purpose. All you need is some sort of external timekeeping device; something you must focus your attention on while your hands are otherwise engaged in the business of picking.

One option could be another human being tapping their feet, clapping their hands, or banging a drum at a steady beat (provided they're capable of such things), or, even better, a guitarist with solid rhythm strumming along. I especially enjoy playing along with drum tracks, where I can play to a beat that I like (check out drumbit.app for the free one I've used often).

Suffice to say, there are no excuses these days for not using one! Which brings us to . . .

BRAINJO LAW #5: Test for automaticity by playing alongside an external timekeeping device.

You can apply this law to virtually anything new that you're learning, whether it's early technical skills on your instrument, a difficult section in a new piece, or an entire song.

With this fifth law established, we can create a foolproof and basic procedure to guide the pace at which we learn any new technical skill on our instrument, which is:

1. Practice the new thing until it gets easier, then

2. Test for automaticity by playing along with an external timekeeping device

If you fail step 2, you just go back to step 1 and repeat the process.

If you pass step 2, then you can move to the next item in your learning agenda with the confidence that you've effectively carved out yet another pathway and are one step closer to molding your musical mind.

5

LEARNING WHAT CAN'T BE TAUGHT

. . . .

Have you ever been to a concert where a musician gets the crowd clapping along to the beat? I'll bet you have. And you've surely noticed how quickly everyone syncs up with the music.

Research tells us that by the age of three or four, virtually everyone can find and match the beat in a piece of music after just a few seconds of listening. This ability is formally known as "beat induction," in case you need to impress your friends.

Now, imagine someone asks you, "Teach me how to clap along to the beat." What would you say? It'd probably be something like "I have no earthly idea!" Or imagine if you had to write a computer program that could identify the beat in a song without any drums or percussion.

If that sounds like a formidable challenge, then you're in good company. It's a problem that stumped the top minds in computer science for decades. Not coincidentally, it was only solved when we developed machine learning algorithms modeled after the brain. The computers learned it themselves, which means we still don't understand how it's done!

Needless to say, there's a whole heck of a lot going on underneath the hood, so to speak, when you're clapping along to the beat. Yet, you can do it effortlessly. And you can do it even though nobody ever taught you how.

Now, when you hear the phrase "you can't teach that," what does it mean to you? It's a phrase you hear all the time in sports commentary, uttered when a player does something unique or remarkable. But you also hear it in other domains, like music. And the implication is that the individual displaying the skill that "can't be taught" was born with it.

Of course, when you stop and think about it, this makes zero sense. In case you've never come across a brand-new human, I've got news for you: they are totally inept. They aren't even born with the ability to hold up their heads, roll over, or control their bodily fluids. They are so inept, in fact, that they require full-time care and supervision by other humans just to stay alive.

And yet, it *is* true that there are things—a great many things— that can't be taught. Nobody taught you how to talk. Nobody taught you how to walk. Nobody taught you how to tell the difference between the expression of fear and surprise, or anger and disgust. Just like nobody ever taught you how to find the beat. We learned all our most advanced cognitive abilities with zero formal instruction! Nonetheless, the idea that we are born with certain talents and abilities persists.

If you see someone clapping along to the beat, you are entirely correct if you say, "you can't teach that." But here's the catch: you'd be entirely wrong if you said, "you can't learn that." The critical misconception here is that skills that can't be taught can't be *learned*.

The misconception has fueled the myth of innate talent. It's the reason why, to this day, many people still think there's such a thing as a "musical" or "nonmusical" person. Consequently, many give up on pursuing their musical dreams if they lack certain skills. By this line of thinking, if you don't currently possess the kinds of innate musical abilities that "can't be taught," then trying to learn music is a waste of time.

WE'RE ALL "SELF-TAUGHT"

I'm sure you've heard people marvel at accomplished musicians who were "self-taught," meaning they never took formal lessons with a teacher. But the truth is that we are all self-taught because nobody can implant knowledge and skills into our brains. We must acquire these things for ourselves. What a good teacher or system of instruction *can* do is to help us create the best conditions for that to happen.

For example, if you want to teach a child how to ride a bike, explaining to them Newton's laws of motion and the movements of the body and feet that are needed to maintain balance are not going to help them learn how to ride a bike (not that you could accurately describe those things).

And yet, it's very likely that, if you're able to ride a bike, somebody helped you in that process. What did they do? They provided your brain with the conditions where it could discover how to move your muscles to maintain balance.

Oftentimes, providing those conditions is a matter of simplifying the task in some way so that the learner can focus directly on taking the next step in their learning progression. But again, it's a step that only they can take. And in the end, everyone ultimately teaches themselves how to ride a bike, even if they had someone who helped make that process easier.

Remember the First Law of Brainjo: To learn to play like the masters, we must *learn to play* like the masters. Anyone who has mastered a musical instrument has done so not by virtue of innate ability, but because they provided their brain the environment needed to learn what couldn't be taught.

Unfortunately, most music instruction doesn't provide any guidance on how to do that. Instead, it typically focuses on the things that can be easily articulated, like where to put your fingers to make a D chord, how to hold an instrument, or the notes of the major scale, while neglecting critical auditory skills like pitch matching, chord identification, rhythm and timing. Yet, without those skills, progress hits a hidden barrier. Every time.

BRAINJO LAW #6: Acquiring musical fluency requires learning what can't be taught.

Years ago, when Brainjo was first conceived, my goal was to create a system of instruction that would provide a reliable path to musical fluency. I knew that doing so would require a deep understanding of how to learn the skills that can't be taught. Understanding how to acquire those skills for myself became a top priority, as did understanding how to help others do likewise. Much of that involves understanding how to harness and leverage the immense computation power in our subconscious networks, which is the engine of all complex learning.

6

THE EASIEST WAY
TO GET BETTER

. . . .

When it comes to pattern recognition, the human brain is king. Compared to the rest of the animal kingdom, our brain's ability to extract patterns from the world around us is arguably its single greatest distinguishing feature.

It's what enables us to make accurate predictions about our world, and to imagine new tools and technologies. And it does all this in the service of one primary goal: *to keep us alive*. The better our brain can predict and manipulate the world around it, the better its odds of achieving that goal.

But here's the wondrous thing about our pattern recognition capabilities: most of it occurs beneath our awareness. In other words, it happens without any conscious effort or deliberation on our part, and it happens whether we even want it to or not.

Just going about the business of our day, we provide our brains with a continuous stream of sensory data that it sifts through and analyzes in an effort to better understand the world we inhabit.

This isn't the narrow view of learning most of us are accustomed to. Most of us have come to believe that learning is something that requires teachers, books, and intensive study. And to be worthwhile, it probably should be a bit unpleasant.

Yet, most of the knowledge that any card-carrying adult member of the human race possesses wasn't acquired in this way. Most of it comes simply by existing in this world and trying to become a functioning human, and it starts the moment you draw your first breath.

Every six-month-old knows that if they drop their bottle, it'll hit the ground with a pleasing thud. We all implicitly understand the law of gravity long before we ever crack open our first science text.

When you see someone's face with their eyebrows and mouth angling down and their eyes narrowed, you immediately recognize the face of anger. You can interpret all sorts of facial expressions, in fact, effortlessly and instantaneously.

Yet how many times have you sat down and analyzed the differences between patterns of facial muscle contraction and the emotions they convey? Not once, I imagine.

LISTENING TO LANGUAGE

Nowhere are our pattern circuits on more impressive display than in the process of learning our native language. It is the crowning achievement of human cognition and, to this point, an achievement unique to our species. Most children are fluent by the time they enter their first school classroom.

In order to reach fluency, the child's brain must be able to decode the composite sounds of speech, build associations between those sounds and the concepts they represent (e.g., that the sound for "cheerio" refers to the crunchy little circle Mom puts on their plate every morning, etc.), and then construct motor programs that allow them to reproduce the full array of those sounds through the vibration of their vocal cords, coupled with movements of their mouth and throat.

Now, next time you have a conversation with a three-year-old, ask them how they figured all that out. They'll surely cast a quizzical glance in your direction. *Figure out what, exactly?*

Here we have the most sophisticated of human behaviors, the pinnacle of human cognition, and it develops without any formal study whatsoever. The brain, using its massive computational horsepower, figures it out for you using nothing more than the data of daily experience.

Now, how can we put this remarkable pattern recognition ability we already possess to good use when learning banjo? Preferably with zero effort?

By *listening*.

Let's revisit the infant learning how to talk for a moment. The first rudimentary attempts at spoken language don't typically begin for a full six months after birth. What, then, is she doing in those preceding six months? Being a bit lazy, perhaps?

No. She's *listening*.

In order for her to utter the sounds that comprise her native tongue, she must first know what those sounds are. She must unravel the basic sonic units of her language.

And this is no trivial matter. Nowadays, you're so good at parsing through the sounds of your native speech that you probably take this gift for granted. But to get a glimpse of just what a major feat this is, simply listen to a conversation in an unfamiliar language. It's entirely inscrutable. You don't know when one word stops and another begins because you've never built the neural structures needed to do so.

The very first task our language-learning infant must conquer, then, is to build a vocabulary of the fundamental sonic building blocks of her language. Yet, to do so, all she must do is listen to other humans speak.

She listens, and the amazing pattern-recognizing machine inside her skull does the rest.

Over time, as she begins the practice of making those sounds with her voice, her brain builds associations between her sonic vocabulary and contraction patterns of the muscles that control her mouth and throat. Ultimately, and in impressively short order, she will become an expert at producing those sounds.

And this is precisely the kind of neural machinery we're trying to build as we learn an instrument: associations between sounds in our head and movements of our limbs (so that those sounds come out of our instrument).

As such, the language acquisition model provides us with an ideal template to guide our learning efforts. It's one that Mother Nature has refined over a couple of million years, so we'd be wise to pay attention.

Which brings us to the **Seventh Law of Brainjo:**

BRAINJO LAW #7: Listen often to the sounds of
the music you wish to make.

We're all in the midst of learning a language—the language of our chosen instrument. And, like any language, it is composed of basic sonic elements that combine to make the music we enjoy.

These are sounds that are unique to each and every instrument, and that are further defined by style and technique. So, like the infant learning her native tongue, we must first acquaint ourselves with these sounds if we hope to one day be able to fluently reproduce them on our instrument. What's more, the richer our sonic vocabulary, the more effectively we can express ourselves with our music.

So listen up. Find the music and musicians that move you, the music you'd like to make, and listen every chance you get. Then sit back and let your brain do the heavy lifting.

It's as central to your development as a musician as any other aspect of practice. And it couldn't be any easier.

7

FAILURE IS NOT AN OPTION

. . . .

SKATING LESSONS

Recently, I've been going to the ice-skating rink regularly with my family, as my daughter is taking lessons. And while I do enjoy the actual skating part, perhaps my favorite thing to do while I'm there is to watch the new skaters.

I live in Georgia, a place with a climate that has long precluded a winter sports tradition. Which means each trip to the rink almost guarantees there will be a new crop of folks hitting the ice (pun most certainly intended). For me, they provide another fascinating window into the learning process. What I've found particularly enlightening has been the contrast between the kids and the adults who take to the ice for the first time.

The disparity between the novice child and adult skater could not be more striking.

The new adult skater enters the rink by gingerly placing a foot on the ice, simultaneously maintaining a death grip on the rink wall. This is often accompanied by a face of intense concern, or perhaps blind terror.

On the other hand, a typical new child skater, especially the youngest ones, enters the rink by charging onto the ice with wild abandon. About three or four steps later, they're sliding face-first across the ice.

This behavior typically continues until the end of the session. The newbie adult clinging fast to the wall, baby-stepping their way around the oval with one primary goal in mind: *not falling.* Usually, they succeed. Or they might fall to the ice once, call it a day, and retire to the spectator's bench.

The newbie child continues to try skating as fast as his or her legs will go, falling countless times, all the while smiling and giggling from ear to ear.

By the end of the first hour, guess who's become the better skater? I'll tell you: it's not even close.

LEARNING MACHINES

This contrast between the adult and child learner plays out in virtually any domain. When presented with a new task, each will typically adopt very different strategies. The child will usually explore freely and fearlessly. *Give me that and let me figure out how it works!*

An adult, on the other hand, will often approach a new endeavor with caution and trepidation. *I best be careful, lest I screw up and break something.*

Perhaps nowhere is this disparity more apparent than with new technologies: my son had figured out how to turn my iPhone on and download apps from the App Store by the age of two, for example (which is common for kids nowadays). On the other hand, it took a to-remain-nameless adult member of my extended family years to even conquer her fear of smartphone technology enough to even touch one, and she still requires extensive coaching on its basic functions.

The adult is afraid to make a mistake. The adult's top priority is *to not screw up.*

The child seeks them out. The child's top priority is *to learn.*

If we broaden our perspective, these differences aren't all that surprising. The human brain doesn't fully mature until our early twenties, an eternity compared to the rest of the animal kingdom.

And the reason we have such a long childhood is so that we can grow really large brains. Brains that are customized to the particular environment we inhabit. Brains that will support the full range of cognitive and motor skills that comprise a fully functioning, independent, adult human in that environment.

In other words, the entire purpose of our childhood, from the brain's point of view, *is to learn.* Children, particularly those of the hominid variety, are born masters of the learning process because Mother Nature has designed it this way.

But here's the challenge: our brain must possess neural networks that are suited to a particular environment, but it can't create those networks until it knows what that environment looks like. Our brain has solved this challenge by becoming a general-purpose learning machine, one that can change itself in response to the demands placed on it.

For example, every infant brain starts out primed and ready to begin learning a language of some sort. Yet, it won't know until the first adults around it start talking whether that language is Spanish or Swahili.

Furthermore, creating these customized neural networks from scratch requires feedback. Lots and lots of feedback.

Feedback that says, "you're on the right track," or feedback that says, "this still needs work." And this network-building process is iterative: the brain creates a bit of the network, tests it out, then refines it based on the results.

A MATTER OF MINDSET

So much of our success or failure in learning anything new, whether it's ice-skating or piano playing, hinges on the mindset we approach it with. That voice inside our heads, the one that likes to judge everything we do, can be our ally or enemy. And nowhere can this voice be more to our detriment than when it comes to the necessity of failure.

Those newbie kids at the skating rink, the ones falling all over themselves, have the right mindset. They instinctively know that, in order to grow, they have to fail. The faster the better. Falling to the ice isn't interpreted as a personal failing but as priceless feedback.

The geniuses at Pixar Animation Studios have been able to consistently produce some of the most enduring movies of their generation by following the guiding principle to "fail fast and fail often." They too know that the faster they "fail," the faster they improve.

Whether we're looking to master the art of skating, animating, or banjo-ing, the next Law of Brainjo is essential for getting us there:

BRAINJO LAW #8: There is no failure, only feedback.

8

HOW MUCH SHOULD
YOU PRACTICE?

. . . .

If you hang out around internet banjo forums much, as I've been known to do, you'll notice certain commonly recurring topics:

"What's the best banjo under X amount of dollars?"

"Can I play Scruggs style without fingerpicks?"

"How much do you practice each day?"

Years ago, when I first took up the banjo, I'd find those conversations about practice time a bit demoralizing.

Tales of daily marathon sessions of eight to ten hours were commonplace. Anything less than four and you best not speak up for fear of public shaming.

I was in my first year of medical residency when I got my first banjo, when ninety-hour workweeks were the norm. In those days, I was thrilled if I could squeeze in fifteen to thirty minutes of picking time in a day. Was I deluding myself by thinking I could become a banjo player with such comparatively little time to devote to it?

Needless to say, not only did I become very interested in methods that would maximize practice efficiency at that point, but I also became intensely concerned with the question of how much practice was truly enough.

We seem to have a natural tendency to believe that if a little of something is a good thing, a lot is greater, even if our experience tells us that more is not always better.

So what then of practice? How much is enough? And is there such a thing as too much?

THE MINIMUM EFFECTIVE DOSE

First, let's clarify precisely the question we're asking, which is *how much practice time is necessary to get results?* In other words, what amount of time is required to make sure that the next time we pick up our instrument, we're a little bit better?

Remember, the goal of each practice session is not to get better right then and there, as getting better requires structural and physiological changes in the brain that take time—changes that are set in motion during practice, but that continue long after we've set our banjos down (much of it while we sleep).

With this in mind, our question then becomes, what's the minimum amount of time needed to signal our brain to change?

NECESSARY CONDITIONS

As stated above, to learn anything, the brain must literally remodel itself to build novel neural circuitry that supports the new skill or technique we're learning.

Yet we don't have unlimited space or energy to work with. Our brain is relatively fixed in size, and building new brain stuff requires precious energy stores. To operate successfully within these constraints, our brain must be selective about when it changes, and when it doesn't.

To illustrate, think back to February 9 of this year (or last, depending on the time of year you're reading this). Do you remember what you had for breakfast, lunch, and dinner? Do you remember who all you spoke with that day, and the contents of those conversations? The emails you sent? The websites you visited?

Me neither!

You don't remember those things because your brain didn't deem them worthy of long-term storage. They weren't worth devoting valuable space and energy to. And I think you'll probably agree that your brain made a good decision! Whether it was eggs, toast, or a Pop-Tart on February 9, who really cares?

And how exactly did your brain decide not to encode those things into long-term storage?

Because you didn't pay much attention to them.

Every minute of every day, our brain is busy sifting through an incomprehensible amount of sensory data. Most of it is discarded as irrelevant, not worthy of the resources required to store it for a later day.

But what of the stuff that is worthy and relevant? How does the brain know to keep that for later?

By only storing the things we play close attention to.

Attention is how we tag the events of the day to signal our brain that we might need them again later, cueing the brain to then rewire itself toward that end. There's a large body of research on this issue, and the results are solid: without attention, memories aren't formed, and skills aren't learned.

But the type of sustained and focused attention we're talking about here isn't easy, and it isn't something most folks can carry on for too long in one stretch. At least not before the mind tires and begins to wander. And once the mind wanders, further efforts are wasted.

And what's the typical amount of time a person can maintain attention before their performance starts to degrade? About twenty to twenty-five minutes.

BRAINJO LAW #9: When practicing something new, practice until your attention starts to fade. For most, this will be twenty to twenty-five minutes.

So, if our practice sessions are best divided into twenty- to twenty-five-minute bursts (in particular, ones where we're working on something novel), the next question, then, is whether this is enough time to trigger the brain to remodel itself in the service of our desired skill. Stated another way, how much is enough time to induce neuroplasticity?

Until recently, we were left to only make an educated guess about this question. But thanks to recent technological advances, we now have the tools to assess when the brain has remodeled itself through practice, enabling researchers to target questions of this nature more precisely.

Using those tools, it's been shown that just twenty minutes of focused practice time is enough to produce the structural changes in the brain that support skill acquisition.

I would venture that it's not coincidental that the average time limit of the human attention span and the time it takes to trigger the brain to change itself overlap so closely.

Putting all this together, we can reasonably conclude that, when learning something new, about twenty to twenty-five minutes of focused practice is sufficient for achieving our goal, which is to ensure that the next time we sit down to play our instrument, we're a little bit better. Yes, you *might* could do more, but you don't *need* to do more.

Furthermore, given what we know of the limits of human attention, and given that there's a limit to how much the brain can change in a day, the practice curve is likely U-shaped, like this:

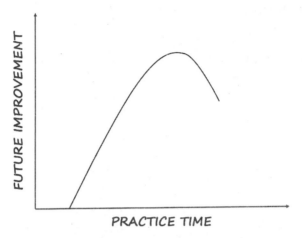

The "U-shaped" Practice Curve

After a certain amount of time and our attention fades, we face diminishing returns. If our lack of focus results in sloppy playing, then our entire session may end up being counterproductive. We can take a break and return later, of course, but at some point we come up against the limits of neuroplasticity.

As is so often the case, quality trumps quantity. Short, high-quality practice sessions are far superior to longer, low-quality ones.

So, should your predicament be as mine was many years ago, when the demands of work and family left little time for banjo plucking, don't despair. Take heart, and keep in mind this next Law of Brainjo:

BRAINJO LAW #10: When practicing new skills on your instrument, quality beats quantity. Twenty to twenty-five minutes of focused, distraction-free practice is sufficient to ensure consistent progress.

9

CAN YOU PRACTICE TOO MUCH?

. . . .

We've learned that when it comes to practice, quality trumps quantity. For triggering brain change, attention matters more than time. As discussed, around twenty minutes of focused practice is enough to stimulate the neuronal rewiring that leads to progress. Furthermore, to ensure we provide our brain with high-quality data to guide its rewiring, we ideally want to stop before our attention fades.

But what if, after you've taken a break and replenished your attentional resources, you *want* to do more? In particular, what if you want to work on something different? Can multiple short, focused practice sessions throughout the day accelerate your progress? Or could they actually undermine it?

CAREFUL DELIBERATION

First, let's clarify that what we're talking about is formally known as "deliberate practice," where our goal is to drive rewiring in the brain. With deliberate practice, we're working on acquiring a specific skill with a clear objective, like seamlessly transitioning between a C and a D chord or nailing a tricky section of a song at eighty beats per minute.

However, not all the time we spend with our instruments is dedicated to deliberate practice. Sometimes we may just want to noodle around without any real goal. In fact, aimless noodling can be time well spent, as that's often where real creative magic happens. Other times, we just want to kick back and play the tunes we know and love, savoring the fruits of our practicing labor. For times like those, there's no need to set time limits. Let your bliss be your guide.

So, to reiterate, the central question relates to practice where we're trying to stimulate and steer brain plasticity to get better at a specific thing. And since our brain has finite resources, it's reasonable to wonder if there's a limit to how much it can grow and change. You're probably well aware that, in the realm of physical fitness, there's a limit to how much muscles can grow in a given amount of time, and that exercising a muscle for too long can undermine growth by stealing resources needed for recovery.

What, then, are the limits for our brain? And how should those limits inform how we practice?

Fortunately, we have scientists who like to answer questions like these! That includes a trio of intrepid researchers who, in 1996, published one of the most influential studies on this topic. The investigators in that study aimed to determine whether practicing a different motor task shortly after practicing a new one would disrupt the neural rewiring triggered by the initial practice session.

At the time of the study, researchers had already demonstrated that a similar kind of disruption occurred with other types of memory. For instance, it was known that if you give someone a list of words to memorize and then, a few minutes later, present them with another list of words, the second list interferes with their ability to recall the first one. This phenomenon is known as "interference."

The question in this study was whether learning two motor skills in close succession would lead to the same phenomenon. In other words, would learning the second motor skill disrupt learning of the first?

To answer this question, the researchers designed an apparatus consisting of a joystick that controlled a computer cursor. The joystick was attached to a metal arm with two joints, which were connected to motors that could adjust the forces on the joints as the subjects moved the cursor. The device was programmed so that the forces changed predictably, allowing the subjects to learn how to move the joystick more accurately with practice. In the experiment, the subjects tried to hit targets on a computer screen with their cursor as quickly as possible.

In essence, the researchers created a device that allowed their subjects to implicitly learn a particular motor skill. Subjects in the control group performed a set of trial runs on the first day and were tested again on the same task with the identical joystick settings twenty-four hours later. The result?

Their performance improved significantly over the course of twenty-four hours, meaning they were better at controlling the joystick after twenty-four hours of rest (including a period of sleep) than they'd been during the previous day. Their brains had rewired after their practice session to improve their abilities on that task (remember Brainjo Law #3: The primary purpose of practice is to provide your brain the data it needs to build a neural network).

In contrast, the test group was given a second trial with entirely different joystick settings after the first trial. This meant that the movements that they'd learned to control the cursor with the initial settings were no longer of use. The test groups performed this second trial with the new joystick settings at different intervals: one group immediately after the first trial, a second group after five minutes, a third group after an hour, and a final group four hours later.

Then, just as they'd done with the control subjects, they tested all the test group subjects on the first task with the original joystick settings. How did the test subjects fare?

The group that performed the second task either immediately, at five minutes later, or one hour later, showed no significant improvement on the original task the following day! In other words, attempting to learn the second motor task shortly after the first one disrupted the learning of the initial task. Unlike the control group, their training did not trigger neuronal rewiring. However, the group that waited four hours did show improvements in the first task, just like the control group.

Furthermore, subjects who waited an hour or less between practice groups also performed much *worse* on the second task compared to those who waited four hours. Back-to-back practice sessions not only prevented them from learning the first task, it undermined their practice of the second task.

NERDS, FTW

What do these findings mean for those of us learning a musical instrument? Let's imagine two people, Jack and Jill, who are both learning the banjo and are equally skilled at it. Their teacher has given them both the same two pieces of music to learn.

Jill, who is well-versed in the phenomenon of motor interference, practices the first piece for twenty minutes and then puts her banjo away for the day. Jack, who thinks neuroscience is for nerds, spends twenty minutes practicing the first piece, takes a ten-minute break to browse TikTok, and then spends twenty minutes practicing the second.

Based on the research, what would we expect their results to be? We would expect Jill to have improved significantly in her playing of the first piece. On the other hand, we would expect Jack to have not improved at all on the first piece and possibly have improved somewhat on the second one.

If Jill continues on this strategy, she will learn her two pieces in roughly half the time as Jack, despite spending half as much time practicing! That's a 400 percent greater return on her practice time, and a prime example of the value of practicing smarter, not harder.

Should Jill decide to practice both pieces in the same day but more than four hours apart, we would predict she'd learn them in a quarter of the time it takes Jack, despite putting in the exact same amount of practice time as him.

This scenario is a perfect illustration of how a little knowledge of neuroscience can go a long way! Since the publication of this study, many others have been conducted to confirm and expand upon our understanding of the phenomenon of motor interference. That includes demonstrating that interference is bidirectional: when two different tasks are practiced with little time in between, the first task interferes with the ability to learn the second (retrograde interference), while the second task interferes with the ability to learn the first (anterograde interference).

Another useful concept that has emerged from this research is the "synaptic modification range." The basic idea is that there is a limit to the amount of synaptic modification that can occur in a given amount of time. Think of those synapses as like a sponge that can only absorb a certain amount of water at a time. Once the sponge is fully saturated, trying to add more water will not make it absorb more. Instead, we need to allow the sponge some time to dry out before it can effectively absorb water again. Similarly, the research suggests that the brain needs at least four hours to "dry out" or reset its synaptic modification capacity before it can efficiently learn a new motor task.

There is a caveat: whether you need to wait depends on whether your two tasks are utilizing overlapping neural circuitry. That's because another important finding from research in this area is that the nature of the task performed also determines whether interference will occur. For instance, if subjects perform the joystick task and are then asked to remember a list of words, interference does not occur. This is likely because the two tasks involve entirely different brain areas and synapses, so there's no competition for resources. In other words, interference occurs when there is synaptic overlap between two tasks.

INTERRUPTING INTERFERENCE

What are the practical applications here? How can we leverage our awareness of the phenomenon of interference to enhance the returns on our practice efforts? Let's translate these findings into some guidelines:

1. **When practicing to learn something new (i.e., deliberate practice), aim for at least twenty to twenty-five minutes of focused practice.** To boost your results, just before you go to sleep, spend a few minutes visualizing practicing it again (more on how to do this in a later chapter).

2. **If you want to practice learning something new in less than four hours, make it in an area that's unrelated.** We can divide the skills needed to develop musical fluency into three categories: technical skills (the movements of our limbs that control our instrument), perceptual skills (our auditory or "ear" skills), and conceptual skills (our understanding of how music works).

   So, if you've spent time working on a technical skill and want to work on learning another skill shortly thereafter, make it from one of the other categories. Spend some time training your ear, for instance, or work on a music theory concept. Doing so will help ensure that you aren't triggering a battle for synaptic remodeling resources.

3. **If you want to practice learning something different in the same skill category, wait at least four hours to do so.**

10

WHEN SHOULD YOU PRACTICE?

. . . .

In the last chapter, we tackled the question of practice time: just how much we actually need to get better, and whether it's possible to practice too much.

This time, we're shifting our attention to a different but related question:

When during the course of the day should that practice take place?

WHAT'S YOUR CHRONOTYPE?

In this modern, newfangled world of ours, with all manner of artificial light sources at our disposal, we're free to set our days and nights according to whatever schedule we please. And if we wish, we can divorce our "daily" routines entirely from the rise and fall of the sun.

Yet, the time that's passed since the invention of the incandescent bulb represents only a tiny blip in the total swath of our history on this planet.

So even though technology affords us the opportunity to escape our ecological niche, our biology remains inextricably linked to the rhythms of nature. Which means that every cell in our body, including those in our brains, still cycles through changes on a twenty-four-hour schedule. These are our "circadian rhythms."

Translation: we operate differently in the morning than we do in the evening, and we're better suited toward doing certain things at certain times of day.

In chapter 8, we discussed the essential role that attention plays when it comes to learning new things. Attention is the means by which we signal our brain that whatever activity we're engaged in, like banjo playing, is worth learning.

And research shows that most humans are able to maintain their sharpest focus in the late morning to early afternoon. This is the time when those attentional circuits so critical for facilitating neuroplasticity are typically at their best. Not surprisingly, given the crucial role of attention in learning, this is the time of day when we tend to perform best at learning new things.

But this window won't be the same for everyone. Your ideal time for practice, the time of day when you're at your sharpest, will in part be determined by your own personal "chronotype," which is just a fancy way of describing whether you're a morning person or an evening person.

As you might imagine, the larks among us are best suited for practice sessions during the early part of the day, while the owls are capable of keen attention far later into the evening.

You likely already have a pretty good idea of which chronotypic camp you fall into. But if you want to get more specific, there's even a quiz you can take to precisely quantify your degree of morning- or evening-ness.

Also, if you start paying attention to the way you feel during the course of the day, the times when you feel your most alert and productive, and the times when your energy starts to wane, you'll realize pretty quickly that this pattern remains pretty consistent from day to day.

BRAINJO LAW #11: The meat of your practice sessions should occur during the time of day when you're at your sharpest (for most, this will be late morning to early afternoon, though this can vary further according to your chronotype).

On a related note, it turns out that our creativity peaks when we're a little bit tired, during periods when our attention tends to wander a bit. This is your best time for free-form noodling, when your random and uninhibited meanderings around the fretboard might lead you to a serendipitous discovery or two that you can add into your bag of tricks.

A WORD ABOUT SLEEP

The primary purpose of practice is to provide our brain with the inputs it needs to wire up new circuits and forge new pathways. And the bulk of that rewiring and path forging occurs during sleep. Sleep is the time for growth and restoration, both physically and mentally.

And there is some evidence that the brain, when it triages the events of the day, gives priority to the activities performed closer to sleep. So, all other things being equal, you may be able to get a little more bang for your practicing buck closer to bedtime.

So, you night owls are in luck. While the logistics of society in general may not be set up in your favor, this is one instance where your contrarian chronotype works to your benefit.

For you larks, who can't imagine mustering the requisite focus for an extended nightly practice session, even just a brief five-minute session to reinforce anything you'd practiced earlier in the day should allow you to still reap the benefits from this phenomenon. Here, all you're trying to do is convey to your brain that you consider that banjo practice from earlier to be a worthwhile thing for it to work on while you snooze.

And you don't really even need your instrument in hand for this condensed, pre-slumber practice. Simply visualizing a brief practice session before you hit the hay should be enough for our purposes here.

If you're not too familiar with the idea of visualization, fear not, as we'll cover it again soon. It's a cheap, efficient, and surprisingly effective tool that definitely belongs in your practice arsenal.

11

THE 3 INGREDIENTS OF AN EFFECTIVE PRACTICE SESSION

· ·

We've covered several important neuroscience principles thus far for enhancing the efficiency and effectiveness of our practice efforts. In this chapter, as a means of reviewing some key concepts and increasing the likelihood you'll apply them, we'll distill our learning into three essential ingredients of an effective practice session.

These can serve as a mental checklist you can run through each time you sit down with your instrument with the intention of stimulating some synaptic remodeling. If all three ingredients are present, you're virtually assured to see a future return on your efforts. Conversely, if one of these ingredients is missing, it's unlikely any rewiring will occur, or if it does, it might not be in the direction you desire.

As previously discussed, the technical term for practice sessions aimed at changing our brain to acquire a new skill is deliberate practice. That's the kind of practice we're talking about here. Research shows that it's not our total time spent practicing or playing that determines how much we improve in a particular skill but the amount of time spent engaged in deliberate practice. If you've made it this far in the book, that should come as no surprise!

That being said, I'm not suggesting you try to obsessively optimize every microsecond spent with your instrument. Rather, my aim is to equip you with the knowledge and understanding to help you move closer to your musical goals, whatever they may be.

ESSENTIAL INGREDIENT #1:
a Clear and Attainable Goal

Every great practice session needs a goal. A crystal-clear idea of the thing that we want to get better at.

It seems obvious that you wouldn't sit down to practice without knowing what it is you want to improve upon. And yet, it happens all the time. I've certainly done it! You may sit down to practice with a general sense that you want to get better at playing your instrument, but you haven't really identified a specific skill that you're trying to improve upon.

When we practice, we want to send our brain as clear a signal as possible of the skill we want it to build. Instead of a generic goal like "get better at music," aim for a specific one like "improve the transitions between the chords for the song 'Long Journey Home' at eighty beats per minute." The more specific your goal, the better. Specific goals not only send a clearer signal to your brain but also ensure that you have clarity on what you need to work on, which requires ongoing and vital self-assessment and reflection.

Being specific in the signal you send is like the difference between calling Domino's and saying, "I'd like to order some pizza" versus "I'd like to order a pizza with half sausage and peppers and half ham and pineapple." The clearer your instructions, the more likely you'll end up getting what you want.

In music, there are three broad categories of skills to learn, and your goal should fall into one of them. It's important to spend time working on skills in each of these categories:

1. *Technical skills.* These refer to the motor programs that control the movements of your mouth, limbs, hands, and fingers needed to make music on your particular instrument. I'd venture that when most people think about practice, technical skills are what first come to mind. Many people refer to this as building "muscle memory," but in reality, you're building "motor system memory" in the brain (muscles don't actually have memories). This is a set of instructions for moving your muscles that is embedded into the substance of your brain.

2. *Perceptual (auditory) skills.* Often referred to as "training your ear," auditory skills are crucial for progressing as a musician. Remember, your ear is really just a lump of flesh optimized for collecting sound waves and can't be "trained" to do much of anything. But we can train our *brain* to learn new auditory skills. The more specific your auditory skill goals, the better. Examples include learning to identify chord changes, match pitches, or find the key of any song.

3. *Conceptual skills.* Often known by the intimidating and imprecise term "music theory," conceptual skills involve understanding how music works and, more important, how to apply that understanding. Specific examples of conceptual skills you might work on with a stringed instrument include using moveable chord shapes, using a capo to play in any key, or describing chord progressions using the Nashville Number System.

STEPPING STONES

As mentioned above, the goal you set should be both clear and *attainable*. At any point in time in your progression as a musician, there are skills that you currently possess and skills that you don't. Unless you're an expert, most of the skills that you don't possess are probably out of reach.

For example, if you've just mastered "Mary Had a Little Lamb" on the piano, it's unlikely you're ready to tackle Chopin's Ballade no. 1 in G Minor. Only a fraction of the skills that you don't currently possess are in the "goldilocks zone"—just enough out of reach to present a challenge, but not so far beyond your present capabilities that they're unattainable. Getting from "Mary Had a Little Lamb" to Ballade no. 1 in G Minor requires many stepping stones. Getting there means always knowing the technical, perceptual, and conceptual skills that are presently within reach.

So, how do you know if the goal you've set is attainable? How can you know if it's an adjacent stepping stone? Generally, if you can make some progress toward that goal during your practice session, then it's an attainable goal.

For example, if you are able to correctly identify the key of the song some of the time, then identifying keys by ear is an attainable goal. Similarly, if you can play a particular section of music cleanly and in time at a specific tempo, at least some of the time, then that's an attainable goal.

If your goal is too easy and you nail it each and every time, it's not a stepping stone; it's a stone you're already standing on. That kind of practice session won't lead to future improvement because you've given your brain no reason to change. Perfection is not the goal of practice since perfection doesn't trigger brain change!

On the other hand, if your goal is too hard and you can't make any progress toward it, your brain receives no guidance on how to change and improve. In this case, the gap between your current capabilities and your goal is too wide, and you don't yet possess the neural structures required to cross it. You must build those structures first.

If you do find that you've inadvertently set a practice goal that's too far out of reach, the solution is almost always to simplify the task. Simplify it by playing slower, removing notes, or making other adjustments until you land in the goldilocks zone.

ESSENTIAL INGREDIENT #2: Undivided Attention

We've discussed this one at length in prior chapters. But remember, attention is the gatekeeper of neuroplasticity. The structural changes in the brain that support learning and memory occur primarily during sleep, and the things that you paid close attention to during the day are what trigger those changes.

Without extended, undivided attention, the brain doesn't change to acquire new knowledge and skills. And as discussed previously, it seems to take at least twenty minutes of practice with undivided attention to trigger the brain to change.

ESSENTIAL INGREDIENT #3: Feedback

To improve, we need to know how we're doing. We must have some way to assess whether we're getting closer to our goal.

In some endeavors, feedback is baked in. When learning to shoot a basketball, there's no ambiguity about how well you did. If the ball goes in, you've hit your goal (pun most definitely intended). If it doesn't, you need to make an adjustment on the next attempt. Furthermore, the greater your miss, the more you need to adjust your next shot.

Importantly, all these error correction calculations and adjustments happen in neural circuits deep in your brain, walled off from your conscious mind. We don't learn to shoot a basketball by consciously diagramming the necessary movements and forces required (not that we could) and following those instructions. Rather, we learn it by repeatedly feeding our subconscious networks the data they need to build and refine a basketball-shooting algorithm. The main job of our conscious mind in this process is simply to direct our attention and behavior to the task at hand so that we feed those subconscious networks.

When it comes to music, your primary tool for feedback are your ears (technically, your auditory cortex). You listen to what you play and evaluate whether you achieved your goal. If you don't, your brain makes adjustments based on that feedback to try to bring your next attempt closer to your goal.

Legendary banjo player Earl Scruggs was quoted as saying that he had no idea what he was doing when he played the banjo, and so couldn't teach someone else how to play like him—a sentiment expressed by many expert musicians.

Similarly, if you were to ask a basketball player to articulate the precise sequence, timing, and force of muscle contractions that are needed for them to make a three-pointer from the top of the key, they would also have no idea. But their brain knows. And their brain figured it out through a great many sessions of deliberate practice laden with invaluable mistakes.

Remember, with music, our ears are our primary feedback mechanism. If we listen intently to the music we make, our brain will figure out what it needs to adjust so that our movements achieve our desired results. Give the brain what it needs and let it work its magic.

MISSING THE BEAT

Now, imagine trying to learn how to shoot a basketball without ever knowing whether your shot went in or not. Would you ever get better? Of course not, which is why feedback is an essential ingredient for a quality practice session. The necessity of feedback seems obvious, yet there's one area in the realm of music where people often do practice without feedback of any kind: rhythm and timing.

Developing solid timing and rhythm is essential to making great music. Playing the wrong note at the right time is seldom noticed, but playing the right note at the wrong time sticks out like a sore thumb. Yet, many aspiring musicians develop shaky timing and rhythm. Why?

While the scapegoat is usually a lack of an innate sense of rhythm, the real culprit is practicing without feedback from a timekeeping device like a metronome, drumbeat, or backing track. If you consistently practice without feedback about your rhythm and timing, you're almost guaranteed to develop shaky rhythm and timing! It's no different from trying to learn to shoot a three-pointer without ever knowing whether your shot went in. In this case, poor rhythm has nothing to do with talent and everything to do with how you've practiced (so always practice with a timekeeping device, especially as a beginner!).

THE THREE CRUCIAL QUESTIONS

To ensure that you have the right ingredients, ask yourself the following questions at the beginning of each practice session. If you answer yes to each, then you have all the ingredients needed to bake some delicious brain change.

1. Do I have a clear, specific, and attainable *goal*?

2. Am I able to give my undivided *attention*?

3. Do I have a clear source of *feedback* to evaluate my efforts?

THE RIPPLES OF PLASTICITY

Sticking an assortment of electrodes onto someone's head allows you to record the brain's electrical activity seeping through the surface of their skull. Gross, I know. This recording, known as an "electroenchephalogram" (EEG), summates the electrical activity of the brain's roughly eighty billion neurons into a single waveform that shows the change in voltage over time. Although it may seem like a crude measure, the EEG has proven a surprisingly useful tool and has long been one of our best ways to measure brain activity in real time.

One fascinating EEG phenomenon that's been discovered is known as "feedback-related negativity" (FRN). While it may sound like a clinical term for your friend who can't handle constructive criticism, FRN actually describes the behavior of an EEG waveform in response to a particular event.

The "negative" in this case refers to the downward, or negative, deflection of the EEG waveform, and the "feedback" refers to the fact that this negative deflection, or spike, occurs about 200-300 milliseconds after a subject has received feedback. The electrical activity itself typically comes from the electrodes stuck to the front middle part of the head (and is thought to emanate from the anterior cingulate region of the brain).

Importantly, the FRN occurs only in response to feedback indicating that we were *wrong* about something. It occurs when our actual outcome doesn't match our intended outcome, including making a wrong movement. For example, if I strike the D string of my banjo while intending to hit the G string, it should generate a negative spike on my EEG recording about 200–300 milliseconds after I become aware of that mistake.

Moreover, the size of an FRN has been shown to correlate with our future performance. The bigger the spike, the more likely it is I will perform better on a future attempt. So, if my brain sends out a big, juicy FRN after picking the wrong string, I'll be more likely to hit my desired string in the future than if it sends out a teeny spike (or none at all).

It appears, then, that what we're witnessing with an FRN are the electrical echoes of the brain's decision to rewire itself. Which, if you recall, is the point of deliberate practice! And what sorts of things produce the kind of big spikes that predict greater rewiring? We've already mentioned that it's triggered by feedback, which is in the name. But we also need that feedback to signify that an error has been made, which means that we also must have a goal to evaluate our results against.

What do you think is the last factor associated with a larger spike? If you said attention, then congrats, you've been paying . . . attention! The greater our level of attention and arousal, the bigger the FRN. The existence of a neurobiological phenomenon that maps directly onto our conceptual framework is an elegant validation of our three-ingredient practice recipe. Bon appétit!

12

THE SECRET TO
STAYING MOTIVATED

. . . .

"Nothing in the world can take the place of persistence. Talent will not;
nothing is more common than unsuccessful men with talent."
—CALVIN COOLIDGE

I recently had a personal revelation. It's something that on some level I think I always knew, but that didn't really reach my full awareness until just the other day. It's a revelation that's expanded my own understanding of my musical life to this point, one that I think holds the key to helping you keep your motivational fire burning strong.

I'll get to that revelation in a minute. First, let me briefly address the topic of motivation, and the vital role it plays in the learning process.

THE MOST POWERFUL FORCE IN NATURE

I don't think much of the idea of "talent." If you've read this far, you probably know this already.

More specifically, I don't think much of the notion that our innate predispositions or aptitudes have much to do with our final results. The research on learning—including research on musical mastery—just doesn't support it.

So if, in the final analysis, talent doesn't matter, then what does? Persistence.

The biggest key to getting better, to moving from a beginner to an expert in any field, is simply the act of showing up every day. Your single greatest ally in your musical journey is not your own unique set of inherited helical strands of deoxyribonucleic acid floating around in your cell nuclei. Nope, your single greatest ally is not your genes but your will to persist.

It's your will to persist long enough so that you can change your brain from where it is now, to where you want it to be. No player who reached the pinnacle of expertise ever got there without being persistent. Doggedly, obsessively persistent.

Simply maintaining your will to keep going, to press onward and to learn new things is the single most important thing you can do to continue to grow as a musician.

Flipping this around, the single greatest *impediment* to continued growth and eventual mastery are the things that sap your motivation to do just that; the things that attempt to thwart your desire to show up every day.

Some days, showing up is easy. Some days, it's all you want to do. If you've been on this earth for any length of time, however, you're used to the natural ebb and flow of your will. Motivation is easy when things are new and exciting, but ultimately the shine and newness wear off, and the surrounding excitement fades.

Puppy love only lasts so long. Eventually, passionate infatuation must be replaced by something more lasting.

With learning an instrument, there's the additional phenomenon related to expertise that you must contend with. In the early days, when you have zero prior skill, your initial achievements feel *monumental*. On paper, going from not being able to play an instrument to playing through your first song from start to finish is likely the greatest musical chasm you'll ever cross. After that, there has to be something more to keep you pressing on.

Every musician experiences lulls in motivation. And for some, the dips become permanent. All those instruments gathering dust in closets and attics around the world bear testament to it.

Sometimes it's because life has gotten in the way, one way or the other.

But oftentimes fading motivation comes from feeling discouraged. And those feelings of discouragement usually stem from one thing: unmet expectations.

In other words, you feel discouraged when you expect to be at one place, but you're not there. Maybe your goal when starting out was to play like a favorite musician, to play a certain complicated song up to speed, or be able to improvise with ease in a jam.

Whatever the case, you had a fixed idea of where you wanted to be one day, and you're not there yet. Maybe not even close. And you wonder whether you ever will be. So you get discouraged.

The problem here, however, isn't your actual skills on your instrument. It's those very expectations that you've set for yourself.

So today I want to show you a better way. A way of viewing your learning process so that those unmet expectations don't happen. So discouragement doesn't creep in, sabotaging your all-important desire to persist.

THE ROOT OF SATISFACTION

So back to that revelation.

The other day, I was reflecting on my life with the banjo, one that began well over a decade ago. In December of 2001 when I received my first banjo, I was a total beginner. If you'd told me then I'd be able to play things I can play now on the banjo, I don't think I'd have believed you. I can play things now that would have seemed impossibly complicated to my beginner self.

But here's the revelation I had recently: my enjoyment of playing the banjo has not changed over the years (i.e., I've always loved it!).

Maybe this seems obvious to you, but it contains what I think is an amazingly powerful truth about human nature. While my skill level has increased exponentially, my satisfaction and enjoyment with the tunes I play today are no greater than the satisfaction and enjoyment I derived from those very first songs I learned. In speaking with other players, I think this is a universal phenomenon. But it's not one you hear about much.

Furthermore, it contradicts the story we often tell ourselves about when we'll feel satisfied with our playing.

Because that story usually goes something like this: one day I'm gonna get really, really good, and *that's when the real fun will begin*. "When I can play like [insert famous Player X], that's when I'll have made it. That's when things get good!" for example.

But the truth, which gets back to that revelation, is that every stage is fun—just as fun as the next, in fact. The idea that once we reach a certain point, we'll be satisfied is an illusion, a fantasy. Not only does it set us up for unmet expectations, but it even sets us up for disappointment once we reach that level and realize that things don't actually *feel* any different.

At first this may seem paradoxical. Surely, I wouldn't enjoy the same sort of thrill I had from those first banjo songs were I to play them now.

So where does that satisfaction and fulfillment come from?

Progress.

The reason every stage has been equally fulfilling is because each new stage meant I'd progressed to some degree. I was playing something on the instrument that perhaps in the prior weeks or months I couldn't. I'd improved, and that felt great.

By itself, simply playing something complicated or advanced isn't where satisfaction really comes from. Satisfaction with your results comes from improving relative to where you've just been.

Even better, if we shift our focus to making incremental progress, we've substituted an outcome that we may not reach for years—the path to which we can't even envision yet—for an outcome we know we can reach, where the path to reaching it is obvious.

"When eating an elephant take one bite at a time."
—CREIGHTON ABRAMS

ONE BITE AT A TIME

Back when I was a beginner, had I been able to see a video of my current self playing, I would've said, "Yes, I'd like to play like that guy one day."

Yet, the irony here is that at that time I'd have had no earthly idea how to get there. It was only by breaking up the process of learning the banjo into mastering manageable, incremental steps that the path forward revealed itself.

The danger of setting your sights exclusively on a long-term goal is that you have no idea how you'll get there. If tonight I were to get in my car and drive from Atlanta to Orlando, I'd see nothing but the few feet of road visible in front of my headlights the entire way. Yet, if I just maintain my focus on staying on that bit of road in front of my car that's lit up by my headlights, I'll end up in Orlando.

I still have to know in advance that Orlando is my final destination. But to successfully navigate that 450-mile stretch, I don't have to know every twist and turn of the road in advance, I just have to focus on remaining on the path I can see in front of me. Furthermore, the way to the next patch of road, the next step in the journey, will only reveal itself once I've cleared that present stretch of road.

If you focus on making attainable, incremental progress, over time things add up. In incredible ways you could've never imagined, until one day you find yourself playing things you never thought possible. But that never happens unless you focus on those small improvements to begin with.

Which brings us to the next Law of Brainjo:

BRAINJO LAW #12: Maintain focus not on an end goal but on making consistent, incremental improvements.

13

WHAT PROGRESS
REALLY LOOKS LIKE

· ·

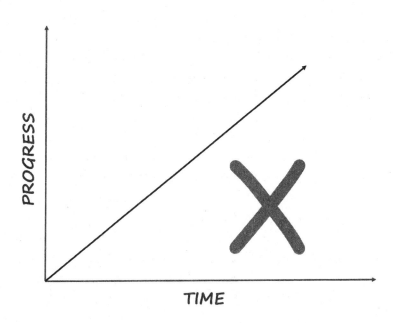

PROGRESS

TIME

I'll bet this has happened to you:

On an ordinary day, just like any other, you pick up your instrument and start plucking around. After a few minutes, though, you note that something isn't quite right. You feel clumsy, you can't pick the strings as cleanly as you'd like, and tunes that typically come easily feel like a struggle.

It's like you've stepped into a time machine and gone back several months, or more.

UNCONSCIOUS COMPETENCE

We've discussed that learning the mechanics of banjo playing requires that we build new pathways, new networks of connections between brain cells that control the various aspects of playing. As our banjo playing skills improve, so do the number and complexity of those networks.

Furthermore, these are *specific* types of neural networks that we want to build, ones that do not require input from our conscious mind for their execution. These learned, unconscious scripts are what power all our complex knowledge and skills. In psychological terms, the development of expertise is about moving from conscious incompetence (executing a skill poorly via effortful, conscious control) to unconscious competence (executing a skill well via effortless, unconscious control).

To progress down the Timeline of Mastery, we want to build a complete set of effective and efficient unconscious scripts for banjo playing, so that our picking becomes *automatic*. Research on neuroplasticity has shown us that, inside the brain, your first attempts at performing a new skill look very different from your attempts after the skill has been fully learned.

At both the cellular and network level, the parts of your brain controlling your first awkward attempts to form the D chord shape, or any other new motor sequence, will look quite different from your attempts after that skill has become automatic. Which means that between those two points in time, a lot of change must happen inside the brain.

LEARNING FAST AND LEARNING SLOW

One helpful way to view skill acquisition is to divide the process into two types of learning, *fast* and *slow*.

Fast learning is, naturally, learning that occurs relatively fast, on the order of minutes to hours. Learning the digits of a new phone number, or remembering how a new melody goes, for example. These sorts of things are accomplished by physiologic changes in the brain that occur quickly, like adjusting the strength of connections between synapses (the region where brain cells communicate with each other).

Slow learning tasks, on the other hand, take longer. They take longer precisely because they can *only* be accomplished by changes in brain physiology that take longer. Changes like the formation of *new* synapses, the sprouting of new dendrites, or even the whole-scale transfer of parts of the network from one region of the brain to another.

These are all processes that require days, if not weeks, to unfold. Just *how* long depends on multiple factors, including the complexity of the skill being learned, in addition to how well prepared the brain is to learn that particular skill. And whether the brain is well prepared depends largely on how thoughtful we've been with our learning sequence up to that point.

Most of the building of the unconscious scripts that power banjo playing involves slow learning processes, which is why the purpose of practice, as mentioned in Brainjo Law #3, is not to get better right there and then but rather to *provide your brain the data it needs to build a neural network.*

And based on what we know of the biology of network building, specifically the varied processes that support slow learning, we shouldn't expect our progress to be in a straight line day to day.

Depending on the skill involved, our progress *might* be day to day, but it very well might take longer.

And during the process of neural reorganization that facilitates slow learning, we're unlikely to see significant improvements. We may even see dips in our performance, periods when it *feels* like we've actually regressed.

But just as you've likely experienced these moments of apparent setbacks, I'll bet you've also experienced the opposite: times where you've struggled with something for a while, perhaps even concluding that it's just too difficult, when suddenly—BAM!—you can do it. With ease, in fact. It's in these moments that your unconscious script, now complete, has just been brought to life (you may have even experienced these moments after several days or more of *not* playing at all).

> *"The three P's of success: Passion, Persistence, and Patience."*
> —DOUG BRONSON

SETTING EXPECTATIONS

In the beginning, your initial gains feel huge because, well, they *are* huge. The chasm between zero skill and being able to play through your first tune is enormous. And, just as the year between your fortieth and forty-first birthdays *seems* a lot shorter than the one between your fourth and fifth, it may feel as if your progress slows a great deal over time.

Furthermore, the longer you play, the better you get, the more sophisticated your mechanics, the more complex the unconscious, automated networks that support them become. And so they take longer to build. Taking longer to build means that the plateaus, or the time between the creation of one network and the next, will get longer. This may give the impression that you're not progressing, even though under the hood, er . . . skull . . . you are.

It could be all too easy to give up in these moments when we feel like we have ten thumbs. But, understanding that these moments may reflect progress in disguise can provide us the all-important patience we need to give things just a little more time.

BRAINJO LAW #13: Expect your progress to look like a staircase, not a straight line.

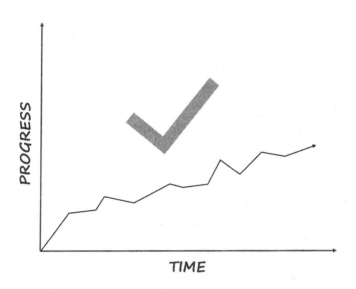

14

MIND OVER MATTER

. . . .

When I was growing up, I wanted nothing more than to be Luke Skywalker. Along with pretty much every other boy I knew.

And of all the cool things Luke got to do, like pal around with robots, pilot a spaceship, shoot lasers, save princesses, and wield a light saber, it was being able to use the Force I most fantasized about.

Using nothing more than his mind, Luke could hurl objects across a room or even lift a spaceship in the air. In other words, he could change things in the physical world using nothing but his thoughts. What could be cooler?

So I spent many an evening staring at my action figures, focusing all my thoughts on launching them across my bedroom.

And . . . nothing.

As the years passed, the limitless possibilities of childhood fantasy slowly faded away, including my Jedi aspirations. I resigned myself to the fact that changing something in the physical world using nothing but my mind was not a realistic goal. The Force, it seemed, would never be with me.

I was wrong.

Multiple studies have demonstrated that many of the benefits of practice, and the attendant changes in neurobiology that accompany them, can be attained simply by *imagining* yourself practicing. Simply thinking about practicing our instrument causes our brain to restructure itself in the same way that actual practice does.

Sound familiar?

In sum, visualization is an incredibly useful practice technique. In fact, as we'll discuss, there are certain skills that visualization develops even better than actual practice.

That said, I also know that if visualization is not something you're used to doing, you may feel a bit lost when it comes to getting started with it. If so, fear not! In this chapter, I'm going to share a simple procedure to help you get started, one I'd say that pound for pound is the most effective way to reap the full benefits of visualization.

MORE THAN A LEARNING SUBSTITUTE

The fundamental idea of visualization in the context of skill learning is to simply imagine yourself performing the skill in question. Some folks may misinterpret this to mean that you should imagine *watching* yourself playing (the name itself is part of the problem, as it implies watching something). This is not the idea.

You actually want to imagine yourself *doing* the activity. You want the first-person perspective, not the third. And you want to be *feeling* what's happening as much as you are *seeing* it.

To ensure that you've got the idea, go ahead and visualize writing your name with your nondominant hand. Or throwing a ball.

In either case, visualizing these things should feel just as awkward as they do in real life. If you can feel that awkwardness when you visualize writing or throwing with the limb you don't usually use for those activities, then you've got the right idea.

As I alluded to earlier, multiple studies have shown that this type of first-person visualization activates many of the same areas as physical practice. In other words, when done right, many of the same parts of the brain that are active during actual banjo playing are active during imagined banjo playing.

In this sense, visualization can be viewed as a substitute for practice when, for whatever reason, you can't pick a physical banjo.

But this view sells the technique a bit short, as there are additional benefits—ones that are somewhat unique to those of us learning the music of an aural tradition—that are actually *easier* to attain through visualization than physical practice.

By definition, when you're visualizing playing music on your instrument, in the brain you're connecting an imagined sound with an imagined feeling—in this case the bodily perceptions that accompany playing.

And, if we consider the types of neural networks that support the skill set of a master musician, this is precisely the thing these networks do. Through years of [the right kind of] practice, the masters have created direct neural mappings between imagined sounds (what they want to play) and movements of their limbs (so that those sounds are emitted through their instrument).

So, when you visualize, you too are building exactly the kind of neural networks that support the highest levels of musical expertise. In fact, you have no other choice. With no notation or tab to look at, no hands to stare at, you've removed the visual system from the equation. All that remains is sound and movement.

Visualization is also a fabulous technique for memorization, and provides a surprisingly accurate assessment of how well you know a tune. If you can visualize yourself playing a tune from start to finish, then you know with certainty that you've committed it to memory. If you can't, then more work is likely needed.

BRAINJO LAW #14: Visualize while listening to your recorded playing to effortlessly build sound-to-motor mappings.

HOW TO START

So, now that I've hopefully convinced you that visualization belongs in your suite of practice methods, here's what I think is the perfect way to get started putting it into action. And it just takes two simple steps.

STEP 1: Record yourself playing.

Ideally, record yourself playing through a tune you're still working through, one that you have yet to satisfactorily get "under your fingers" (you can even just record a section you're finding especially tricky).

Alternatively, and particularly if you're first starting out, you could begin by recording a tune you already know well. Even in this case, you'll be reaping some of the visualization benefits (specifically, building those sound-to-motor mappings I discussed earlier).

When recording, make sure to play through the piece as slowly as you need to in order to maintain accuracy. Speed is of little importance here. And it's fine to look at a tab or some other written source if needed.

STEP 2: Play back your recording at a later time, and visualize when you do.

Now, to practice the visualization part, simply play the tune back at a later time (while away from your instrument), and visualize yourself playing as you listen.

What you'll find is that having an auditory trigger, and having that trigger be something you've already played, will make the visualization part nearly effortless. In fact, most likely the visualization will occur naturally; you almost can't help but imagine yourself playing when listening to a recording of yourself.

And that's it. Record yourself, then listen back later and visualize when you do. Over time, you'll likely reach a point where you can visualize without the recording (and I would recommend periodically testing yourself to see if you can do so).

THE TIME TO VISUALIZE

It goes without saying that one of the great benefits of visualization is that it allows you to practice when it'd be otherwise impossible to do so (in the car, walking around the neighborhood, while exercising, while engaged in unstimulating conversation, so I've heard).

But I think the absolute best time, when possible, is right before going to bed—something I do often (it can even double as a cure for insomnia!).

In a previous chapter, I covered the topic of how to choose *when* to practice. As you know, sleep is the time when we grow. It's the time when the brain does most of its rewiring in support of transforming the experiences of our day into physical memories.

And there I mentioned that the brain, when deciding what of those daily experiences to commit to long-term storage, appears to give priority to activities performed closer to sleep (all those college kids cramming right before bed understand this phenomenon on some level).

Yet, getting in an actual practice session before hitting the hay isn't always the most practical thing. So what better way to still reap the benefits of the sleep proximity effect without having to disturb your family or neighbors than to conduct that practice session entirely in your mind? It's the perfect win-win.

15

THE MEANING OF MASTERY

. . . .

A while back, I had the pleasure of conducting an interview with master banjoist Adam Hurt, widely considered a banjo virtuoso. Part of the conversation centered around Adam's description of his personal style.

Many would describe Adam's playing as "innovative," with a style that pushes the boundaries of clawhammer banjo technique. Given that unique and innovative sound, many would be surprised to learn that he is very much a student of the tradition.

"What I think I do different from a lot of people in the melodic clawhammer banjo camp is I use more traditional banjo techniques to create the melodic turns of phrase that I want," Adam says.

Adam is often lumped into the "melodic" camp of banjo players ("melodic" meaning he likes to play as many notes from the fiddle as possible), which most folks would consider to be a more "modern" approach to clawhammer. And his playing clearly fits the bill.

Yet, his style has always been uniquely identifiable among

other melodic players. A few notes into any tune leaves no doubt who's behind the banjo.

Yes, this is due in part to a machinelike precision of tone and technique. But there has always been something else different about it that previously I couldn't quite put my finger on.

Now I realize what that was, which is the deliberate, thoughtful, and . . . innovative use of traditional 5-string banjo techniques in the service of a melodic approach. This is the thing that made his playing stand out most from the melodic crowd.

LESSONS FROM BANJO CAMP

Back in 2005, back when I was first getting into clawhammer banjo, I attended Suwannee Old-Time Banjo Camp in North Florida. It was an incredible experience in so many ways, and in retrospect a real inflection point in my life.

If you've never been to a music camp before, I highly recommend it. There's something special that happens when people geek out in the woods for days around a common interest. It's doubly great when there are banjos involved.

And they're an amazing—and often overwhelming—learning experience. The focal point of the learning is the classes, but for me, some of the best lessons are learned outside the classroom.

One of the unique aspects of the experience is that, over the course of the camp, you have the chance to get to know the instructors and their distinct personalities a bit.

It was during the faculty concert the final night, after having had the chance to get a least a little sense of who these folks were, that I observed something that would ultimately influence my own concept of mastery, and that would provide a guiding beacon for my own journey as a player from that point on.

Yes, the concert was fantastic. The music was terrific and inspiring, as you'd expect given the lineup of icons of banjo like Mike Seeger, Brad Leftwich, and Mac Benford.

But the thing that stood out most for me about the playing of these master banjoists wasn't their impeccable rhythm and timing. Nor was it their purity of tone or technical sophistication.

The thing that stood out was that, in spite of the fact that they were all playing essentially the same style and drawing from the same canon of musical material, they all sounded very different. More than just different.

They all sounded *like themselves*.

No, I'm not just stating the obvious. What I mean is that their own unique personalities that I'd come to know a bit of over that weekend were now coming out, loud and clear, through their banjos. They'd somehow managed to take a piece of themselves, funnel it through their instrument, and transmit it out into the world.

It's natural, I think, to view mastery as simply the accumulation of technical skill. It's also the easiest thing to measure and quantify.

Yet, there are master musicians whose playing is technically straightforward but moving, and there are musicians whose playing is technically advanced but forgettable.

Carlos Santana could surely navigate the guitar fretboard with greater speed and dexterity than Bob Dylan, yet both are viewed by many as masters. Why? Because they both know what they want to say on their instrument, and have the technical skill needed to say it.

Technical skill, then, is a necessary but insufficient condition of mastery.

It's not about whether you know three hundred tunes by heart, how many notes per second you can play, or if you can solo between the seventeenth and twentieth frets.

It's about whether you've reached the point where you know what you want to say, and you have the chops needed to say it.

BRAINJO LAW #15: Master musicians have found their voice, and have developed the technical skills needed to express it.

16

THE TIMELINE OF MASTERY (AND THE ROOTS OF IMPROVISATION)

· ·

Vowel sounds . . . 3 months
Babbling . . . 6 months
Monosyllabic words ("mama") . . . 9 months
First words . . . 12 months
2- and 3-word phrases . . . 24 months
Uses tone of voice to add additional meaning . . . 3 years
Carries clear conversations with well-developed grammar and articulation . . . 4 years
Fluent, improvisational speech . . . 5 to 6 years

If you're a parent, you probably recognize the above timeline. These are the language milestones of childhood, the stages through which a developing child moves on their way to achieving fluency in his or her native tongue.

Embedded in this chart are two very important messages that most of us know to be true, even if we've never really given them much thought before:

1. **Virtually every child learns to speak to the point of fluency,** or "improvisational speech" (and exceptions warrant investigations into nervous system disease or dysfunction).

In other words, like you, the child reaches a point where he or she is able to effortlessly and nearly instantaneously translate thoughts in his or her mind into a motor program for the vocal cords, in effect turning thoughts into speech in real time.

2. Every child follows this *exact same learning sequence*.

There's no better template than the language learning model when it comes to learning music (though I'd argue it's the ideal template for learning *anything*).

Fundamentally, our ultimate goal when learning to speak and learning to play an instrument is the same: to turn thoughts into movement. In the case of language, we're translating concepts or ideas into the movement of the vocal cords. In the case of an instrument, we're translating musical ideas into movement of the limbs.

But there's one big glaring difference between language learning and musical instrument learning . . .

The failure rate!

Whereas the failure rate for language is extraordinarily small, the failure rate for learning an instrument is extraordinarily high. Especially when you compare the two.

What's even more remarkable about this discrepancy is that

the ability to speak fluently is, if anything, more cognitively sophisticated a task than playing a musical instrument.

So why the difference?

A FOOLPROOF SCRIPT

Clearly, our brain is predisposed in certain ways to learn language from the get-go. Parents know that their children learn their native tongue not through some ingenious and meticulously devised curriculum they've created but almost entirely on their own.

You just bring your kid out in the world, sit back and watch as magical things happen inside their noggins over the next few years. Then one day—voilà!—they're talking back to you!

In this respect we can acknowledge that our brains are tailormade for this language learning business. Language has been so critical to our success as a species that it drove the evolution of our unique cognitive abilities, and so we have neural machinery right out of the gate that helps us learn it.

Yet, there are several thousand languages throughout the world, and our DNA doesn't know at conception whether our language will be Spanish or Swahili. The specific language can't be hardwired by the time we draw our first breath. Rather, it must be *learned*.

So how have we solved this problem of ensuring that every human learns to speak?

By providing the ideal *learning path,* a learning path that, in the absence of disease or deliberate attempts to derail it (i.e., depriving a child of sound), is *foolproof.*

This is what the developmental milestones are telling us. Every child passes through the same milestones in the same order because each step, and the order in which the child moves through them, is absolutely critical to their ultimate success. In a polylingual world, this is how the brain ensures that each human reaches fluency.

What's more, it's assumed that every healthy child will move through this process and become an effective speaker. There's no anxiety about whether or not he or she is gifted enough to learn to do it. It's just a matter of building up one component skill sufficiently, then moving to the next. While the end result is extraordinary, the process itself is plodding and mundane.

And there's no real urge to rush the process. We know it doesn't make sense to start teaching a six-month-old how to write poetry in iambic pentameter, nor to become discouraged if he or she can't carry on a conversation on the finer points of the quantum wave function at the age of one.

A MATTER OF TIME

The most wonderful thing about the human brain is that its capacity to learn, to remold itself in response to environmental demands, remains throughout its life. And this, of course, includes our brain's capacity to learn music.

The only difference is that, unlike with language acquisition, our culture no longer provides the ideal learning environment for every child. But the principle remains: follow the right path, and success is virtually inevitable. And there's no skipping ahead, no rushing to the advanced material before the early stuff has been mastered.

Just as every language-speaking human passed through the same language milestones, you'll find the same to be true of musical masters. Though the speed with which they did so may have differed, they all passed through the same sequence in their own pursuit of mastery.

So at this moment, eradicate all talk of "bad" and "good" players, musically talented or not, etc. These concepts are useless at best, destructive at worst.

The difference between someone who can play through two tunes at sixty bpm and a master who can play freely in a jam has nothing to do with these sorts of things. It simply has to do with their current location on the Timeline of (musical) Mastery. One is further along, but the journey can be had by anyone who chooses to walk down the path.

Is the typical four-year-old child a more talented talker than a babbling infant? Of course not. It's an absurd notion. One child is just further along on the Timeline of (language) Mastery.

17

FEELING YOUR WAY TO
MUSICAL MASTERY

. . . .

If you're in the business of running a commercial chicken hatchery, it's important to be able to tell the male chicks from the female chicks. Turns out that doing so isn't as easy as you might think.

As David Eagleman recounts in his book *Incognito: The Secret Lives of the Brain,* it takes a good bit of practice to become an expert "chicken sexer," requiring the ability to identify small details in the business end of a baby chick.

Back in the 1930s, the world's most expert chicken sexers were in Japan, and aspiring sexers from around the world traveled there to learn from the best. But here's the odd thing: the expert chicken sexers couldn't actually tell anyone how they did it.

They'd learned their craft simply by *observing* other expert chicken sexers. They'd just watch the experts sort, and over time would learn to do it themselves.

They couldn't describe how they did it. They did it all *based on a feeling*.

WHERE THE MAGIC HAPPENS

Up until quite recently, the scientific community had downplayed the importance of feelings in the realm of human cognition. Feelings were treated as the redheaded stepchild of the mind's inner workings, viewed largely as a holdover from an earlier phase in our brain's evolution. Feelings arose from an ancient, more primitive part of the brain, and so couldn't always be trusted.

Our thoughts, on the other hand, were the product of the rational deliberations of our conscious mind. Thoughts were the crowning achievement of human intelligence.

Not so fast.

If there's one consistent theme that's emerged in the last decade or so of cognitive science research, it's that the most remarkable feats of human cognition aren't the product of, nor are they even *understood* by, our conscious mind. The reason why an expert chicken sexer can't tell you how he or she sorts a baby chick is because his conscious mind, the part that does the talking, *doesn't understand it, either.*

We've talked in prior chapters about the importance of listening in the music learning process. That while we listen, subconscious pattern detectors are busy crunching the auditory data, extracting out useful bits of information that will then inform our future playing. All this while our blissfully ignorant conscious mind just sits back and enjoys itself.

But if so much of our cognitive activity isn't the domain of the conscious mind, how does the subconscious ultimately influence our behavior?

Through *feelings.*

The subconscious bits are always working, always busy crunching the bits and bytes of the day's sensory data. But it's only when those computations turn up something meaningful that the conscious mind becomes privy to their machinations. When those computations *do* lead to something important, it bubbles into the conscious mind as a feeling.

A feeling that then influences our behavior.

For example, when the various compounds in plant matter are chewed, digested, and then analyzed in the gustatory centers, the ultimate output to the conscious mind is a feeling—if it tastes good, then it's likely a good source of nutrition or energy. If it tastes terrible, best not to swallow, as it may be poisonous.

FEELING YOUR WAY TO MASTERY

Finding sources of musical inspiration is a critical component in the journey to musical mastery, as virtually every master's story will attest. Nobody gets very far in isolation.

Number one, finding sources of inspiration is great for keeping your motivational fire burning. Chances are that's why you wanted to learn to make music in the first place.

But as your technical foundation solidifies and you shift to the business of creating your own style, those sources also provide a stylistic storehouse from which you can borrow and steal. Before you can find your own voice, you must first figure out what you like.

And so seeking out and identifying these sources should be a part of every player's journey. But how exactly do you find the best ones? How do you find the ones that'll make the biggest difference in your own story?

By following your feelings.

It's easy to be seduced by feats of technical wizardry, especially lightning-fast fingerpicking that's explicitly designed to impress. "Wow, I can't believe he can play like that. Maybe I can impress my friends and family with skills like that one day." It's easy to think that this *should* be the ultimate goal.

But resist those calls. Appeals to the intellect or ego wear thin, and rarely sustain anyone for the long haul.

On the other hand, when you hear a player that makes you *feel* something—be it happy, sad, excited, or just . . . *alive*—pay attention. Better yet, take notice AND store it away so you can continue to revisit it. Whatever you do, don't downplay or trivialize the importance of those feelings.

As you grow, continue compiling your own library of sources that connect with you in this way. Those are your gold mines. This is the music you connect with most deeply and will serve as an unending reservoir of inspiration.

Not only is this the more sustainable approach, but your audience will appreciate it, too (even if that audience is just you).

The stuff that makes you feel shouldn't be viewed as something *lesser than* the stuff that appeals to your rational mind, as the above discussion illustrates. Those feelings are your brain's way of calling your attention to the very best of what's out there.

BRAINJO LAW #16: Pay close attention to other musicians that make you *feel* something, and study them.

18

HOW TO BUILD AN IMPROVISATIONAL BRAIN

. . . .

In chapter 16, I introduced the concept of the Timeline of Mastery, the learning sequence through which anyone must pass as they develop expertise in a subject.

The gold standard for this type of thing is the timeline of language learning. It's the most reliable and efficient model for human learning ever created. And, fortunately for us, the many similarities between language and music mean there's tremendous insight to be pulled from this model for our own learning purposes.

When it comes to language, the ultimate destination, the marker of mastery, is fluency. One way to define linguistic fluency is the ability to take ideas in mental space ("thoughts") and translate them into speech, in a manner that both seems and feels instantaneous.

Fluency can also be described as "improvisational speech": the ability to take the building blocks of language and connect them in combinations that allow for the expression of ideas that are novel, personal, and specific to a situation.

And this is also about as perfect a definition for fluency on a musical instrument as I can imagine. A fluent musician can take musical ideas in mental space and translate those—seemingly instantaneously—into the sounds of an instrument.

With the language learning model as our guide to improvisational fluency with music, what then would be considered the prerequisites for linguistic fluency? What are the neural networks that must be created to support this skill?

IMPROVISATIONAL NETWORKS

The neural networks required for improvisational speech are:

1. A sufficient vocabulary of words, stored as sonic representations, so that mental concepts can be communicated accurately.

2. Knowledge of the rules of language (grammar), so that the words are assembled in ways that others can understand.

3. The ability to emit all the words in that vocabulary via the coordinated contraction of the muscles of articulation.

In the brain, we know that all of this involves the sophisticated and mind-blowingly complex communication among billions of neurons distributed across multiple, dynamic neural networks.

Generally, these networks and their interactions can be represented as follows:

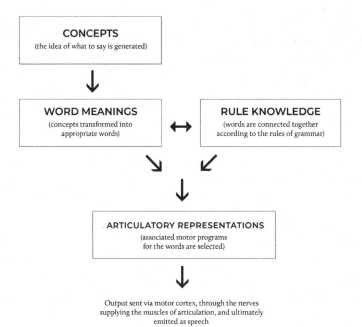

If we wish to create similar neural machinery inside our noggins that will ultimately support musical fluency—then we'd be wise to pay attention to how these networks are built.

How then do you build a really big vocabulary of words?

By reading, and by listening to others who you think are good communicators. Much of this happens just by living around other fluent humans.

How do you build a big vocabulary of musical ideas?

Once again, by listening A LOT, especially to the people whose music you enjoy most.

How do you learn the rules of language? Again, much to your grammar teacher's dismay, you also did this by listening. You listened, and the three-pound master pattern detector inside your skull figured it all out.

How do you learn the rules of music? By listening to lots of music.

When you listen to music, your brain finds the patterns in those sounds, and learns the rules for how it's all put together (regardless of whether you're consciously aware of or can formally articulate those rules). In some cases, formal study of those rules can further enhance your understanding of those rules, expanding the scope of what you can express on your instrument (just as knowing the rules of grammar can, in some cases, make you a better writer).

How do you learn to emit the sounds of language through the muscles of articulation? By practicing, in logical sequence, the articulation of the sounds of language, beginning with the most basic and simple to produce phonemes (the oohs and aahs of those first cooing sounds of a three-month-old) and moving to ones of increasing complexity, followed by syllables, words, and phrases.

How do you learn to connect music in the mind to movement of the limbs? By practicing taking music that you imagine in your mind and emitting it into the world through the movements of your limbs. Just like a child learning a language, the key is to start with the simplest sounds, or building blocks, and work your way up to higher levels of complexity.

Here we have the meat of the learning process for music, the stuff we do when we say we're "practicing," and, not coincidentally, largely the focus of this book. And this corresponds to the third network in the summary table below:

A mature network of this nature, the kind that can support the type of fluency described earlier, is one that can map musical ideas onto the motor programs that control the muscles of the arms—output that produces the coordinated contractions that result in those musical ideas coming out through your instrument.

BRAINJO LAW #17: Musical fluency and improvisation are predicated on the ability to map musical ideas (and the neural networks that represent them) onto motor programs.

Musical, and improvisational, fluency ultimately requires two primary components:

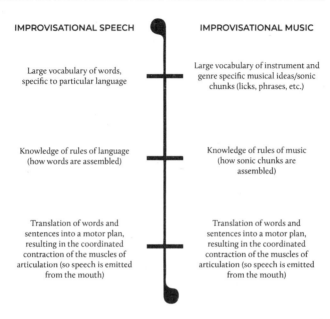

NEURAL NETWORK MODULES FOR IMPROVISATIONAL SPEECH AND MUSIC

IMPROVISATIONAL SPEECH

Large vocabulary of words, specific to particular language

Knowledge of rules of language (how words are assembled)

Translation of words and sentences into a motor plan, resulting in the coordinated contraction of the muscles of articulation (so speech is emitted from the mouth)

IMPROVISATIONAL MUSIC

Large vocabulary of instrument and genre specific musical ideas/sonic chunks (licks, phrases, etc.)

Knowledge of rules of music (how sonic chunks are assembled)

Translation of words and sentences into a motor plan, resulting in the coordinated contraction of the muscles of articulation (so speech is emitted from the mouth)

1. The ability to conjure pleasing musical ideas in one's mind.

2. The ability to realize those ideas in real time on the instrument.

So if developing the neural networks that support fluency primarily involves copious listening and the development of instrument-specific motor skills of increasing complexity, is there still a role in all of this for written music in the learning process?

19

IS IT SAFE TO USE TAB?

. . . .

Note to the Reader: For those unfamiliar, tablature is a system of notation used for stringed instruments like the guitar and banjo. In other words, a written form of notation. This chapter explores the pros and cons of using written notation of any kind (which of course may include standard musical notation) when the objective is to ultimately learn to play by ear.

I was awoken, as I was well accustomed to, by the dreaded sound of my pager.

The year was 2004. The time . . . 2:30 A.M. I was three years into my residency training, and on this night, I was the on-call neurologist for two hospitals.

"Hey Dr. Turknett, I've got a really interesting case for you," said the voice on the line.

Nothing is interesting at 2:30 A.M., I thought, *except my pillow.*

I was speaking with the night-shift doctor in the Malcolm Randall VA ER, and he was clearly better adapted to middle-of-the-night conversation than I. "Can I just run this case by you? I'm not sure what to make of it. It's probably nothing."

"Sure, what's up?"

"Well, he says he can't *read*. He tried to pick up a book tonight and couldn't read any of it. But here's the strange thing, his vision is *perfectly fine*. And he has no problems talking, no slurred speech or anything. You ever heard of anything like this?"

"It just started tonight?" I asked.

"Yep."

"I'll be right there."

My examination indeed confirmed what the ER physician had reported. The patient, G.R. (as we'll refer to him), was having trouble reading (more specifically, he was having trouble applying the rules of phonology). But, as the ER doc said, his vision was otherwise fine, as was his speech.

I knew this was bad.

My concerns were confirmed by a CT scan of G.R.'s brain, which showed a bright blob on the lower right-hand side of the image. G.R. had bled inside his brain, at the juncture between the occipital and parietal lobes in the left hemisphere, a place where symbolic visual information is decoded. Things like written words on a page, for example.

Despite our technological advances, cases like these still form the backbone of our understanding of human cognition. The specific ways in which brain function degrades when certain parts are taken offline offers us a unique and powerful window into how the brain is organized, and how it processes information.

This includes much of what we know about our gifts for communication, including speech, reading, and writing—information we can use to our advantage as we try to build a musical brain.

Information that can even help us to answer the question of whether tab has a place in the learning process.

More on G.R. in a bit.

THE ORIGINS OF WRITTEN MUSIC

"The map is not the territory."
—ALFRED KORZYBSKI

Just as we humans were talking long before we were writing, humans were playing music long before we started recording that music in written form. Research indicates we've been making music for at least fifty to sixty thousand years, but likely much longer. Yet, our system of written notation has only been used for a few hundred years. Which means that, for most of human history, music was solely an aural tradition, passed along from one person to another entirely by ear. Humans are quite capable of learning music without any written notation whatsoever.

And when we finally did decide to create a written system of musical notation, its primary purpose was for the *preservation and dissemination* of music. Up until that point, music only existed in the human mind. Notation was the only way musical information could be stored *outside* the human mind, as recorded media (the Edison phonograph) didn't develop until a few thousand years later.

Just as writing was developed as a way of *storing and disseminating* knowledge and information for later retrieval, musical notation was likely created to perform a similar function (rather than as a system for teaching).

Later on, when composers needed a way to coordinate large numbers of musicians in a symphony orchestra, they turned to written music to do the job. And so if you were a musician with your sights set on playing in said orchestra someday, then you'd better learn to read that written music yourself.

But somewhere along the way, perhaps because we were able to record music in writing long before we could record the actual music, learning by reading music became the accepted way music was taught. In the days before records, tapes, CDs, and iTunes, the only way to easily disseminate a tune to thousands of ears was to *write it down.*

Times, of course, have changed.

We no longer need to write music down as notation to store it. Furthermore, as a means of transmitting musical information, written notation is an inferior tool for doing so when we now almost always have access to the real thing.

Written notation for a piece of music *is a representation of the thing,* while a recording of a piece of music *is the actual thing*!

THE POTENTIAL PERILS OF TAB

Those of you who've followed along in this series know that we attain new skills through the creation of skill-specific neural networks in the brain, and those networks are built through practice. We have the ability to mold our brains to our own specifications.

While this remarkable feature holds great promise and potential, it also means we must take care in ensuring the networks we create actually do the thing we want.

Let's consider an example.

Jack has just bought his first banjo after having dreamed of playing it for many years. He's motivated and ready to learn and sets a goal of playing in his first jam in six months.

He gets down the basic techniques of banjo playing, and then sets about to start learning some tunes. He finds a book of tablature, and gets to work, putting a couple of hours of practice in every day.

Several months go by and Jack is making serious progress. He can play about twenty tunes up to speed, though he still has trouble playing through a tune without the tab in front of him.

His wife, once dismissive of his newfound interest, remarks that he's sounding pretty good. Buoyed by her encouragement, he decides it's time to venture out to his first jam.

Disaster strikes.

Within a few minutes, Jack realizes that he's in way over his head. Even when tunes he knows come up, he can't keep up, and can't manage to play anything that sounds remotely like music.

He leaves dejected and demoralized. The banjo is retired to the closet, where it remains collecting dust for the next decade.

BUILDING IT RIGHT

In prior chapters, we've reviewed the type of neural networks that support the playing of a master banjoist: networks that efficiently translate musical ideas into a motor plan for moving the limbs (so that those musical ideas are emitted as banjo sounds). We can refer to these as "sound-to-motor" networks.

Banjo playing networks built exclusively through the use of written music, on the other hand, operate quite differently. These networks translate *visual* information into movement of the limbs (so that the written code is translated into banjo sounds). We can refer to these as "print-to-motor" networks.

So, the print-to-motor neural network that Jack has diligently built over many months relies upon tab for its operation. What's more, no neural routes to playing independent of tab exist in Jack's brain, making it biologically impossible for him to succeed in a jam!

Jack didn't fail because he's a bad musician, he failed because he built neural networks that weren't in line with his goals.

REVISITING G.R.

G.R., the patient with the brain hemorrhage that rendered him dyslexic, couldn't read because the hemorrhage destroyed the neural networks that convert the printed word into movement of the vocal cords.

As stated earlier, cases like G.R.'s reveal the functional organization of the human brain, in this instance showing us that there are segregated language networks of various types, each with its specific function, each created through a specific kind of practice. G.R., like most of us, could speak fluently long before he ever attempted to decode his first written word. Before reading instruction ever began, he already had neural networks that could transform mental concepts into movements of the vocal cords.

And it was only when that reading instruction began that he started forming the print-to-motor networks that could translate markings on a page into movements of the vocal cords.

This segregation of function explains why he could suffer a stroke that obliterated one linguistic skill (his capacity to read) but left another (his ability to translate thoughts into speech) intact.

So what exactly does this type of knowledge tell us about the role of written music in the learning process? It tells us that if we wish to create sound-to-motor networks like the master players, then we should avoid incorporating musical notation into our banjo playing networks.

It tells us that we want to build banjo playing neural networks that operate independently of tab.

ARE WE TABBED OUT?

So if we don't want tab incorporated into our banjo playing networks, does this mean we need to abandon it altogether? Does tab have any place in the learning process at all? Is there a way to use it responsibly?

No. Yes. Yes.

While our ultimate goal may be to build networks that can translate musical ideas into motor programs of the limbs independent of printed music, it is entirely possible to use tab, or other forms of written notation, as an *aid* in that process. Most important, tab can be an invaluable learning tool, ideally suited for conveying certain kinds of information.

Years ago, after hearing several of country blues guitarist Mississippi John Hurt's tunes performed by a guitarist at a local farmer's market, I became enamored with John Hurt. After that performance, I soon built up a library of Hurt's music, and set about to learn some of his material.

I soon found that things weren't as simple as they seemed, and I struggled at first to figure out exactly how he was getting those sounds out of his guitar. Then one day I stumbled across a tab for one of his tunes ("Stagolee"), and suddenly it all made sense.

Just seeing that one tab was all it took to unlock the mystery of his style. In a matter of minutes, my eyes were able to unlock a pattern that my ears could not, even after hours and hours of listening. The result was a giant leap forward in my learning process.

Tab in and of itself is neither good nor bad. It's only in the way in which it's used that determines whether it hurts or helps. I use tab a good bit in the Brainjo teaching materials, but the Brainjo Method itself is designed so that the student develops banjo playing neural networks that are independent of it. In my experience, it's entirely possible to get the best of both worlds.

So there's absolutely no reason to abandon tab altogether, provided you are mindful of the way in which you use it, and practice in ways that promote the creation of sound-to-motor networks that exist independently of it. Here are some strategies for ensuring that you do so:

1. When learning a tune from tab, get your eyes off it as soon as possible.

2. After you've learned a tune, visualize yourself playing through it while away from your banjo.

3. Listen, listen, listen to lots of music. As your skills grow, imagine yourself playing along while listening. What would you play? How would you play it?

4. Pick out tunes by ear. Start simple and build this skill. Start with picking out simple melodies (just the basic melody itself, not a banjo player's arrangement of it). Then start working on creating your own arrangements from that melody.

5. Practice jamming (without any written music). Attend a local jam, or just practice along with recorded tracks.

BRAINJO LAW #18: Musical notation (including tab), when used wisely, can be a helpful aid in the learning process, provided that you practice in ways that don't incorporate it into your playing networks.

20

WHY ANYONE CAN (AND SHOULD!) LEARN TO PLAY BY EAR

. . . .

To those who do it, playing by ear may seem as effortless as breathing. To those who don't, the prospect may seem as far off as the Andromeda Galaxy. To many folks, the ability to play by ear is seen as a natural gift. And if you weren't born with the gift, then you're stuck with learning by tab or notation.

This, of course, is nonsense.

OUR EXTRAORDINARY EARS

Let's start with a brief overview of how our ear, or more specifically, our auditory system, accomplishes its primary task of transforming vibrations of air molecules into a rich and detailed sonic experience. To begin with, all sound starts as a wave of air pressure set in motion by the vibration of a physical object.

Once that vibrating air reaches our head, it bounces around the cartilaginous folds of the pinna (the part of the ear you can see), where it is concentrated and then funneled into the dark tunnel of the external ear. Once the air molecules reach the end of that tunnel, they bounce up against the tiny tympanic membrane, also known as the "eardrum." Deflections of the eardrum are then transmitted and amplified by way of three tiny bones that make up the middle ear.

The last of these bones, the *stapes,* transmits these vibrations to an even tinier membrane known as the "oval window." On the other side of the oval window lies the cochlea, a snail-shaped chamber filled with fluid and lined with hairlike projections known as stereocilia. Vibrations of the oval window generate a fluid wave inside the cochlea, displacing the stereocilia and triggering the firing of a neuron—this is the moment when those vibrations of air are finally transformed into neural code.

That neural signal is then relayed through the base of the brain and into the auditory cortex, where it is parsed, distributed, and analyzed, the end result of which is your sonic experience of the world around you.

To help you fully appreciate this analytical feat, imagine yourself sitting in your living room listening to one of your favorite jazz albums (or whatever your favorite genre might be). With virtually no conscious effort, you can easily distinguish the sound of the piano, bass, trumpet, saxophone, and drums.

If your significant other speaks to you while the music is on, you have no difficulty identifying his or her voice, and you have no trouble distinguishing it as separate from the music. Meanwhile, all those extraneous environmental noises you're not particularly interested in at the moment are automatically filtered out as "background." If pressed, however, you could almost surely determine their source and location.

Yet, as you've just learned, all this sonic information is transferred from the world to inside our cranium by the beating of air molecules against the tympanic membrane. Incredibly, this exquisitely detailed, information-rich sonic landscape is created by the brain from nothing more than the deflections of a drum less than a centimeter in diameter.

THE PROCESS DEMYSTIFIED

Let's now contrast what our auditory system does during the course of its normal operation with what it must do when you play a musical instrument by ear. In a nutshell, here's the basic procedure for playing by ear:

STEP 1: Hear a pitch in your head (i.e., in "mental space").

STEP 2: Match it to a pitch that comes from your instrument (i.e., in "physical space").

Musical pitches are vibrations of air molecules that oscillate at *regular* intervals (or "frequencies"). Compared to the *irregular* vibrations that comprise most of our sonic environment—sounds that we decode with ease—musical pitches are much simpler. From the standpoint of complexity alone, then, the cognitive procedure required to decode everyday sounds is more sophisticated than what's required to match pitches in physical and mental space.

Now, guess what? If you sing, you've already demonstrated that you are capable of performing the basic cognitive procedure for playing by ear. You've demonstrated that you can match a pitch that exists in mental space to one in physical space. The only difference in the case of singing is that the pitch is generated by the vibration of the vocal cords instead of the vibrations of the sound-making parts of an instrument.

I can hear some of you now exclaiming in hopeless resignation, "I can't carry a tune to save my life!" If so, I have good news: the very fact that you know you can't carry a tune with your voice means that you have an ear capable of discriminating differences in pitches!

After all, how else would you know you couldn't carry a tune if you were unable to determine that the note you sing doesn't always match the desired note in your head?

Your problem is not that you can't hear differences between pitches, it's that you haven't fully developed the ability to adjust your vocal cords so that they vibrate at the desired frequency. Not to worry, though, because when you play an instrument, this part of the process is taken care of for you (provided your instrument is in tune!).

So we've established that your ear and brain, in the course of their normal operation, already accomplish auditory processing feats more advanced than playing music by ear. And we've established that a great many of you (both singers and those who know they can't sing!) have already demonstrated that you possess the tools required to play by ear. Is there anyone out there who is truly incapable of playing by ear?

CONGENITAL AMUSIA

Congenital amusia, commonly known as "tone deafness," is the inability to discriminate between musical pitches. Like color-blind males whose brains are incapable of distinguishing different wavelengths of light (typically those in the red-green spectrum), those with congenital amusia cannot tell the difference between certain frequencies of sound waves.

These are the only folks who can make a legitimate claim to not being able to play by ear. But just how common is tone deafness?

Congenital amusia runs in families, an observation that indicates it is at least in part genetic in origin (in fact, the very presence of such a genetic condition supports the idea that we are hardwired to discriminate pitches). The uppermost estimate of the prevalence of congenital amusia in the general population is 1.5%, though some experts argue that the actual number is even lower than that.

Yet, even at 1.5 percent, the odds are heavily stacked in your favor. Moreover, most folks with congenital amusia don't find music particularly enjoyable, and so aren't likely to take up an instrument or buy books to help them learn it. Thus, the percentage of folks who are both learning to play an instrument *and* tone deaf is likely much, much smaller than the estimated 1.5 percent.

If we put all of this together, we find the odds that anyone reading this book right now suffers from congenital amusia and thus is incapable of playing music by ear are extraordinarily low. But, if in spite of the preceding discussion you *still* doubt your capacity to learn music by ear, you can go to brainjo.academy/earquiz to take a test for tone deafness.

Contrary to what many may believe, playing by ear is not a natural gift. It is a *learned skill.* Sadly, it's a skill many never even try to learn, thanks in no small part to the natural gift myth. But, rest assured, with rare exception it's a skill that anyone can develop through hard work and practice.

Now, your next question might be, why would I want to do that?

What are the benefits of being able to play music by ear?

Before we go any further, let me remind you that I'm not claiming that musical notation, in whatever form it might be, is not useful. As we've discussed, notation can be a wonderful tool, with many uses that are beyond the scope of this discussion.

Learning to play by ear doesn't mean you must swear off all written forms of music for the rest of your life—in fact, they can function as a helpful aid in the learning process.

That said, depending on notation exclusively might hamper you in ways you may not fully appreciate. The obvious limitations of a notation-only approach are that you'll remain dependent on written sources for learning new tunes, and on-the-fly improvisation is out.

But it can also obstruct your progress in ways that are a bit subtler. For those of you who are currently notation-dependent, see if any of the following scenarios sound familiar:

1. You play a tune flawlessly at home, but it falls apart when you attempt it in a jam.

2. You'd like to add variations to the way you play a tune you've learned from notation but find it nearly impossible to deviate from the arrangement you learned.

3. You find it challenging to play through tunes from memory, without the notation in front of you.

What's to blame for these roadblocks? Let's take a look at the relevant neuroanatomy find out.

YOUR BRAIN ON NOTATION

Here's a rough synopsis of what happens in the brain when you learn a tune entirely from notation. First, light reflecting off the page of music enters your eye and strikes the retina, stimulating photoreceptors there that transduce the electromagnetic energy into nerve impulses. Those impulses are then relayed on to the visual cortex in the back of the brain where a rudimentary image is first decoded.

Once this happens, the image data is then relayed to sophisticated association networks that extract meaning from it. After the written symbols are deciphered, the information is then sent forth to motor planning areas in the front of the brain where a movement plan is rendered.

To execute that plan, nerve impulses are delivered to the primary motor cortex, down through the base of your brain and spinal cord, into peripheral motor nerves that trigger the coordinated firing of the muscles that control your fingers.

If all goes well, the result is an accurate sonic reproduction of the printed music. Through this process, the symbols on the page have been transformed into banjo music using your brain and body as the conduit.

With practice, you might get quite good at this notation-reading procedure, eventually reaching a point where you can play through a tune as you read it. This occurs thanks to the creation of tight, notation specific mappings between the visual and motor cortices (i.e., "see this, do this" connections).

Notice, however, that something is conspicuously absent from the aforementioned neural procedure for playing from notation: *the sound!*

Though the outcome of this process was music from your instrument, your brain got you there without needing any sonic representation of the music whatsoever. Your auditory cortex—the part of your brain that deals in sound—wasn't involved in the making of the music. A bit odd, right?

With this in mind, those roadblocks mentioned earlier make more sense.

Why is it difficult to play a notation-learned tune in a jam? Well, it goes without saying that when playing music with others, listening is essential. Odds are we can't just plow through the tune exactly the way we play it at home with no regard for what the other musicians are doing. On the contrary, to fit in successfully with others our brain must adjust the motor output to our hands *based on what we hear.*

Yet, if we've excluded the hearing parts of our brain when we built our banjo playing neural networks, then we lack the needed neural machinery to make those adjustments. This isn't some deficiency of musical ability; it's simply a natural neurobiological consequence of learning methodology.

And why is it so hard to memorize a notation-learned tune? Memorization without the benefit of auditory input is also a very tall order. To memorize a tune from notation alone, you basically have two options:

1. **Memorize the entire notation visually.** Save those with photographic memories, this is quite hard.

2. **Memorize the entire sequence of movements in the left and right hands.** While easier than the first option, this is still a challenging task. Not to mention it's no fun!

Worse yet, these types of memories are both harder to form and more liable to degrade over time.

So if the neural networks built from a notation-only approach are limiting, what kind of networks would serve our needs better?

IT'S CHILD'S PLAY, REALLY

The ability to communicate with our voices is so important to our species that our brain has evolved to be a master at learning it. And given the many parallels between language and music, childhood language acquisition provides us with an ideal model to emulate.

Consider then how a little girl learns to reproduce the sounds of her native tongue.

To begin, she listens intently to every word uttered by the people around her, slowly building a repository of sounds that are specific to her language. Then she begins to try to reproduce those sounds using the muscles that control the mouth, tongue, chest, and larynx (the vocal apparatus).

These initial attempts at language are crude, but with practice become increasingly sophisticated. In just a few years, she's mastered the sounds of her language. Through the aforementioned learning process, she has built an extensive library in her brain of correspondences between chunks of sound and movements of her vocal apparatus.

These sound-to-motor mappings are so efficient that they are able to almost instantly translate her thoughts into speech. Furthermore, with these elements in place, learning how to say a new word is usually as simple as hearing it once.

Not surprisingly, almost all players who have achieved musical mastery have followed a nearly identical path. It's a path that also begins with copious listening—this time to the sounds of the musical language they wish to speak. Oftentimes, they've spent long periods of time in immersive musical environments. Through this intent listening, a repository of genre-specific (e.g., bluegrass, jazz, punk, etc.) sounds is constructed.

Initial attempts to reproduce these sounds on an instrument are rudimentary and uncoordinated, but with practice become increasingly sophisticated and efficient. Eventually, through this learning process, an extensive library of correspondences between chunks of sound (aka "licks") and movements of the hands is formed in the brain.

In the master musician's brain, these sound-to-motor mappings are so efficient that he or she can almost instantly translate imagined musical sounds into movements of the hands. With these maps firmly established, learning how to play a new tune (and memorizing it) is as simple as learning how the melody goes.

Remember, virtually everyone has a brain capable of playing music by ear, even if the prospect of it seems daunting. With a little patience and persistence, however, you may one day find yourself wondering how it ever seemed so.

21

THE SECRET TO PLAYING FASTER

. . . .

Note to the Reader: You'll note that this chapter singles out banjo players for their desire to play fast. While this group does seem to be uniquely afflicted with speed envy, learning to play faster is a universal concern among all aspiring musicians. So don't let the banjo-centric nature of this chapter mislead you to think it's not applicable to your concerns if the 5-string is not your chosen implement of musical merriment. Additionally, if you've ever been dissuaded from learning banjo because you thought playing that fast would be too hard, this chapter should divorce you of that notion.

Though a universal concern among all aspiring musicians, it's a question that comes up with the banjo perhaps more than any other instrument:

"How can I play faster?"

In this chapter, we'll be zeroing in on the musician's need for speed, why it's such a common concern, and the best way to go about getting it. The answers may surprise you!

MORE THAN MEETS THE ~~EYE~~ EAR

So just why is it that, for so many aspiring banjoists, speed is such a pressing concern, especially in the world of 3-finger style (though the topic certainly comes up among downpickers, too)?

Why is there such an epidemic of speed envy among budding banjoists? Because to the average listener, banjo playing sounds *fast*.

For many, the very first impression they have upon first hearing a banjo being played is one of *speed*. The notes are moving by so quickly that it can be difficult to even comprehend what's going on.

But, as any seasoned 3-finger picker will tell you, much of this is an illusion. The perception of speed has more to do with the style in which the banjo is played than it does with any superhuman feat of finger flicking.

For one, there's the fifth string itself. One of the commonalities among virtually all styles of 5-string picking is the continued plucking of the fifth string. Without it, we wouldn't create the droning sound that's such a signature feature of our beloved ax.

But that fifth string drone is an extra sound you don't hear on most other stringed instruments. That alone gives the impression that something more is going on.

On top of that, there's also all those extra notes banjo players put in between the melody notes. Most styles of 5-string picking involve playing melody notes interspersed with harmonizing banjo sounds, the "decorations" we play around all the notes. In many cases, there's more decoration than melody. If you were to take any banjo arrangement and strip away everything but the melody, it would sound downright tortoise-like in comparison, even without altering the tempo.

This is true of many instruments and styles of playing. It seems like there's a lot going on, but there's an organizing structure beneath it all. Breaking that structure down into its fundamental components simplifies things. A lot.

And all those extra notes on the banjo further enhance the illusion that the music on the banjo is being played fast. Which means for you the player, even when sticking to pedestrian tempos, your typical listener will still be left with the impression that you're tearing it up.

For the beginning banjo player yet to fully grasp the nuances of the style, it can be tempting to conclude that the reason your playing doesn't sound quite right is because it's just not fast enough.

But this is almost *never* the case.

Now that I've hopefully thrown a splash of cold water on your lust for speed, let's examine the issue at hand: Just how does one develop the ability to play faster?

To answer it, we naturally need to first talk about dental hygiene.

BRISTLING WITH SPEED

I'm sure the vast majority of you reading this are well accustomed to the act of brushing your teeth [insert requisite British joke here]. In all likelihood, it's something you've been doing most of your life [expound further on the joke here if desired].

Yet, you didn't always know how to do it.

Brushing your teeth is a *learned behavior* with a specific and stereotyped set of movements that unfold in predictable sequence from start to finish. The whole thing seems trivial to you now, I'm sure, but if you've watched a young child learning it all for the first time, you'll note there's a bit more to it than you may now appreciate.

You grab the tube of paste, unscrew the cap, turn the faucet on (cold side) to wet the bristles, turn it off, align the tube with the brush, squeeze a set amount onto the brush, and so on. There's rather a lot going on!

For a young child who has yet to master it, it's quite a bit to remember and master.

Now, imagine I were to ask you tonight to brush your teeth twice as fast as usual. Could you do it?

Sure, you might feel a bit stressed, and your dentist would surely protest, but nonetheless I imagine you could still ramp up the speed of the whole affair with little effort.

But what about the young child who still hasn't learned it all? What would happen if we asked him or her to double their speed? A faster performance? Unlikely!

In the child's case, each step in the act still requires conscious deliberation, and trying to speed that up would, if anything, likely have the opposite result. More than likely, it would just increase their error rate (sound familiar?), resulting in an overall *longer* time to complete the task correctly.

The reason you can increase your speed easily and the young child can't is because you've fully learned the entire behavior to the point where it is *automatic*. As a result, you can move through the whole sequence while your conscious mind is preoccupied with something else. For the child, on the other hand, *each step still demands their full attention*.

In learning parlance, the adult has moved from the beginning state of conscious incompetence ("I can't do it and I must concentrate hard when I try") to unconscious competence ("I can do it all with my conscious attention focused elsewhere").

In the brain, the neural networks that control these behaviors (formed through the learning process) have become compact and efficient, and are now housed primarily in neurons that exist beneath the cortical layer (subcortical).

And it's this shift into the final stage of learning, and the attendant changes in neurobiology that supported it, that allowed you to increase your speed at will. As a result, you can double your speed, even though you never once worked directly on fast teeth brushing.

Being able to brush your teeth faster was a natural *byproduct* of learning the skill well. It happened as a byproduct of working on other things, without your ever having to work on it directly.

So, then, what would your advice be to a young child looking to improve their own teeth brushing speed?

PLAYING SLOW TO PLAY FAST

Whether it's teeth brushing or banjo picking, the advice is the same. The ability to play fast happens as a natural byproduct of the learning process, or learning the mechanics of banjo picking so that you can play automatically, without thinking about them. Once you've reached this stage, speed comes naturally.

This concept is also embedded in the mantra that's emphasized in music conservatories: "The secret to playing fast is playing slow." Work on proper mechanics and timing at the speeds that allow for it, preferably with an external timekeeping device, and ultimately increasing speed is trivial.

BRAINJO LAW #19: Speed develops as a natural byproduct of a solid learning process.

Before we wrap up, I'd like to put one more dagger in the heart of the musician's need for speed—a final plea in the service of banjo public relations.

If you happen to find yourself pining for a few extra bpm, please remember that playing a song faster does not make it better. In fact, playing it faster in many cases will make it worse.

And playing fast for the sake of playing fast *always* sounds worse.

So banish all egocentric motives for speed. Choose the tempo that allows you to best showcase the song you're playing. Play to entertain, not to impress.

Let go of your need for speed, and speed will find you.

22

THE SECRET TO MEMORIZATION

. . . .

You're gathered in a small circle with a handful of other musicians at an old-time jam, playing traditional fiddle tunes. Only one of your jam-mates is a fiddler, but he's a seasoned one. As the one responsible for carrying the melodic line on each tune, he's leading the show.

Which means if he doesn't know the tune that's called for, then it won't be played.

This will be a short jam, you think. Once you exhaust his repertoire of tunes, you'll have to call it a day. Maybe you'll make it an hour, tops.

But an hour passes, and you're still playing music. Two hours. Then three . . .

Amazingly, this fiddler seems to have an endless supply of tunes he can call forth at will.

"How about 'Molly Ate a Woodchuck in the Pigpen'?" suggests the guitarist.

"Ooooh, haven't played that one in years. How's that go?"

"It starts out dada da da dad—"

"Got it!" he interrupts, and off he goes.

How is this possible, you think. *I've been learning music for a couple of years now, and only know about ten tunes by heart. This guy knows hundreds, maybe thousands of tunes. Is he some kind of musical savant?*

For the uninitiated, seeing a veteran musician call forth a seemingly endless supply of tunes can be a mind-blowing experience. And the natural conclusion is to assume you're witnessing a superhuman feat of musical cognition.

Yet, this sort of thing is not that unusual at all. In fact, most master musicians possess a vast library of tunes they can call up at a moment's notice.

But how on earth is this possible? Most early players struggle mightily to remember just a few tunes. How could this memorization ability gap be so large? Does achieving mastery of an instrument also magically impart an exponential expansion in one's memory?

Before we sink our teeth into the realm of musical memory, let's first consider, for the sake of comparison, another domain of artistic expression: painting.

THE EXPERT ADVANTAGE

Imagine two different individuals, Pierre and Brad. Pierre is an expert painter. Brad is a complete novice. Both are given an assignment to re-create a work by a master artist. Only they're not allowed to look at the original painting when doing so. Rather, they must paint it from memory.

Pierre studies the painting for a few minutes, then begins work on his piece. In short order, he produces an impressive re-creation of the original.

Brad, on the other hand, is a bit overwhelmed by the task. *I have no idea how to paint all this,* he thinks.

Then, to his delight, he discovers that there exists a video of the original artist painting the picture he must re-create.

I don't need to know how to paint at all, Brad reasons. *If I can just copy all his movements, mine will turn out like his!*

So Brad begins studying the video with the goal of committing to memory every stroke of the brush that was made to produce the work he must copy. But soon, with the full magnitude of his task finally sinking in, Brad abandons this approach. There's no way he can commit all of this to memory, he realizes.

Brad looks at Pierre's work and is astonished to find that, to his eye, it's almost indistinguishable from the original. Mouth hanging wide open, Brad wonders how on earth Pierre achieved such a feat of memory.

TAKING THE EASY ROAD

Brad's idea, in theory, wasn't a bad one. The surest way to re-create the original work of art *would* be to make *exactly* the same movements that the original artist made in painting it.

The problem, as I'm sure you recognize, is that pulling this off would require a feat of memorization beyond anyone's capabilities. This just isn't the type of memory the human brain excels at. It's a logical, but entirely impractical, idea.

Yet, Pierre *was* able to re-create the painting from memory. How? By using an entirely different approach.

Through a lifetime spent mastering the art of painting, Pierre has acquired an expansive artistic vocabulary of concepts (house, tree, forest, etc.), along with the motor programs required to translate those concepts into images on the canvas.

If we diagram out Pierre's pathway from recall to painting (the boxes representing function-specific neural networks), it looks like this:

ROUTES TO MEMORY

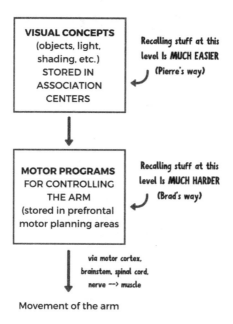

VISUAL CONCEPTS
(objects, light, shading, etc.)
STORED IN ASSOCIATION CENTERS

Recalling stuff at this level Is *MUCH EASIER*
(Pierre's way)

MOTOR PROGRAMS
FOR CONTROLLING THE ARM
(stored in prefrontal motor planning areas

Recalling stuff at this level Is *MUCH HARDER*
(Brad's way)

via motor cortex, brainstem, spinal cord, nerve --> muscle

Movement of the arm

Remembering images, especially those that could exist in the real world, is something we're all quite good at. Take the following painting, for example:

After only a short glance, you've already extracted (whether you tried to or not) the relevant details from it. You know there's a cottage, a forest, a lighthouse, an ocean. You also know their relative locations, along with the time of day, the color of the sky, and so on.

You're able to take the vast body of experiential knowledge you've acquired about the world you live in and use that as a powerful memory aid. You can remember the scene using high-level concepts (lighthouse, cottage, etc.), creating a scaffolding upon which to hang your memory of it.

Pierre can use this type of conceptual memory to his advantage when trying to re-create the original work. Brad cannot.

OUR MUSICAL MEMORIES

Now let's turn our attention to musical memory.

Imagine I was to hum to you a short song of eight measures, with four notes per measure (thirty-two notes in all), and then ask you to hum it back to me. Most would find this to be a relatively simple task.

Now imagine I were to give you the names of each note in this song, which would be a string of thirty-two letters, and then ask you to recite them back to me. Most would find this a nearly impossible task, as the average individual can remember five to seven items.

From the perspective of the amount of information you're being asked to retain, these tasks are similar. In fact, you could argue that the information content is higher in the first example of recalling the melody (especially if you're able to link pitches to their note names).

Yet, the first type of information—a melody that conforms to the rules of Western music—is something every human brain is much better at remembering.

The second type of information—a string of thirty-two letters—is hard for anyone to remember.

Yet, they both represent the same thing. And therein lies the secret to our master musician's seemingly superhuman powers of recall.

A HAPPY ACCIDENT

Earlier, we came up with a definition of musical fluency, the mark of a master musician:

BRAINJO LAW #17 Musical fluency and improvisation are predicated on the ability to map musical ideas (and the neural networks that represent them) onto motor programs.

Like the master painter who, through years of [the right kind of] practice, has built up a library of neural mappings between visual concepts and motor programs for controlling a paintbrush, the master musician has done something analogous, mapping musical phrases onto motor programs for playing a musical instrument.

In both cases, the creation of these networks allows the fluent artist and musician to tap into a type of memory that we're all quite good at: remembering a real-world image in the former case, a melody in the latter.

Yet, these routes to memorization are biologically inaccessible to the novice painter or player.

The development of fluency transforms memorization from something arduous (remembering the movements of a brush or the notes on a page) to something natural and effortless (remembering a scene or a melody).

Before fluency has developed, the only possible avenue you have to memorize a tune is to commit the tab or the movements to memory. And this feels hard because it is hard! For *everyone*.

It doesn't get easier one day because your memory gets better. It gets easier when you begin to develop fluency (as defined above).

Here, as with the ability to play faster, the ability to memorize new tunes easily occurs not through any sort of dedicated memory practice but rather as a byproduct of the creation of brain circuits that support musical fluency.

Which is why building those circuits is the key to mastery.

BRAINJO LAW #20: To exponentially increase your musical repertoire, develop musical fluency.

23

THE "LABYRINTH" PRACTICE TECHNIQUE

. . . .

I need your full, undivided attention for this chapter. Because the practice technique I'm about to share with you is too important for you to miss. It's super simple yet will exponentially increase the efficiency of your practice time.

But first, a story.

FAMILY-FRIENDLY COMPETITION

My son recently had a birthday, and one of the gifts he received was the game Labyrinth. Labyrinth is an actual, physical game that you can touch and feel and exists entirely in the analog realm of real life. A refreshing departure from the land of ones and zeroes that little boys spend much of their time in these days (who am I kidding, it's the land we all spend too much of our time in these days!).

You may have seen or played it. It consists of a movable wooden board mounted inside a box. On the board is a maze, and your job is to navigate a metal ball through the maze, using two rotating knobs that adjust the pitch of the board, without it falling into any of the many holes in its way.

My son soon became obsessed with it, playing one round after another, getting better with each repetition. And then he put down a challenge: "Dad, see if you can break my record." Challenge accepted.

I got to work. Initially, my progress was swift. *I'm going to break his record in no time,* I thought.

Not so fast.

I'd reached the same little section of maze my son had yet to successfully move through, and couldn't get past it despite multiple attempts. Each time, I'd put my ball at the starting point, meticulously guide it through the initial sections, only to have it repeatedly fall each time into the same hole in the maze.

And each time that little section of maze defeated me my frustration grew, as I'd have to repeat the tedious task of starting back at the beginning, then carefully navigate through the parts I'd already mastered just so I could try my hand at that one section I'd yet to conquer.

And then I had what at the time I thought was a revelation.

Why don't I just place the ball at the start of the section that I can't get past, and just work on that one spot until I master it?

That's just what I did. With my enthusiasm renewed, after about six or seven attempts on just that one section, I learned the required maneuvers of the knobs and could consistently make it through. All that was left to do was to set my marble back to the beginning, proceed to the section I had now mastered, and break my now . . . ahem . . . eight-year-old son's record!

Now, I was patting myself on the back for discovering this little shortcut for getting better at the game—which in retrospect seemed kind of an obvious thing to do—when it occurred to me that I do this exact same thing when practicing the banjo *all the time*. It's a technique that seems obvious in retrospect but, just like in the game of Labyrinth, is often overlooked.

So now I'll demonstrate the "Labyrinth" Practice Technique applied to the banjo with a specific example.

HOW TO USE THE LABYRINTH PRACTICE TECHNIQUE

STEP 1: Identify the difficult spot in the tune.

Recently I was learning the tune "Sailor's Hornpipe," and trying to emulate Bill Keith's classic 3-finger version in clawhammer style. Bill Keith was a pioneer of the "melodic" style of 3-finger playing, and so I wanted to incorporate some of the signature picking patterns into my version—patterns that I wouldn't typically play.

And I noticed that, as I was working up my arrangement, I was consistently tripping up at one particular spot that used one of those unfamiliar patterns. It was clearly my weakest link in the entire arrangement, just like the one section in Labyrinth I couldn't get past.

So, rather than play through the entire tune over and over again, the bulk of which I could play just fine, I instead implemented the Labyrinth Practice Technique by focusing my energies on *only* that section.

One of the unique features of the melodic style on the banjo is that notes that are higher in pitch are often played on strings tuned to a lower pitch. If you've been playing stringed instruments for any length of time, you've trained your brain to expect the opposite to be true. Consequently, your brain will strongly resist your trying to execute such a maneuver. Playing a phrase that violates that expectation means having to overcome that resistance, which is why this phrase was especially challenging for me.

STEP 2: Play the difficult section along with a timekeeping device, slowly.

The next thing I did was start up the metronome and find the tempo setting where I could actually play through this section cleanly and with good timing. This turned out to be sixty bpm, roughly half of the final "performance" tempo.

STEP 3: Gradually increase the tempo of the timekeeping device until you reach performance speed. Once I could consistently play through the section at that initial tempo, I increased the speed a bit, working on it again at that tempo until I could play through it consistently. I repeated this process until I reached performance tempo.

Once I'd done so, I knew I could now confidently play through the entire arrangement.

SMARTER, NOT HARDER

There's no telling how long it would've taken me to beat that tricky section in the Labyrinth game had I painstakingly taken my marble back to the start of the maze each and every time it tripped me up.

Like I said, all of the maze prior to that point I could make it through just fine. Had I continued in this manner, I'd have been spending most of my practice time rehearsing something I already knew how to do. Doing it this way, I was only spending a small fraction of my practice time working on the thing I actually needed to learn.

Worse yet, the fact that I had to start over each time and navigate through the sections I'd already learned made each failed attempt all the more frustrating. That frustration undoubtedly worsened my concentration and performance, further reducing my practice quality!

So I encourage you to keep this technique top of mind, particularly when encountering a challenging section of a new piece. Rather than avoid those parts that you find most difficult, go right at them. You'll save countless hours of practice time while turning your weaknesses into strengths.

The Labyrinth Practice Technique is yet another illustration of the principle that *how* we practice is more important to our success than *how much* we practice. If you were to take two people of equal skill and have them try to learn the same piece of music or navigate through the labyrinth maze, and only one had access to this practice technique, I know who I'd bet on to learn it first.

BRAINJO LAW #21: When encountering challenging sections of a new tune, use the labyrinth practice technique to improve practice efficiency.

HOW TO SCARE
AWAY STAGE FRIGHT

. . . .

You've been practicing diligently and are pleased with your progress.

Tunes that once seemed almost insurmountable are falling under your fingers.

Yes, the time has come to share your music with others.

Yet, when it comes time to do so, everything falls apart. Someone who has never held a musical instrument has decided to inhabit your body, just to remind you what public humiliation feels like.

How is this possible? you wonder. You'd had dozens of perfect rehearsals. How on earth could you play so well by your lonesome, and so badly when others are within earshot?

If the above scenario is at all familiar to you, I've got news for you: ***you're a human.***

I don't think there's a musician on the planet, no matter how accomplished, who hasn't encountered stage fright in one form or another at some point in his or her career. Conquering it, at least in part, is critical to any professional musician's success.

If you've experienced it, whether playing for friends, family, an instructor, or a gig, it can be both frustrating and demoralizing. Sometimes the disparity between what you're able to play in the privacy of your home and in public is so great you wonder if you're delusional—are you just listening with rose-colored hearing aids when nobody's around?

So what to do? Do you just accept this as an inevitable part of your nature? Are you doomed for your best playing to fall on no ears but your own for all your days?

Or is there something you can do about it?

The answer, fortunately, is yes (otherwise this would make for quite a boring piece). And it turns out the answer has to do with releasing your inner zombie.

WHO'S DRIVING THE BUS?

Imagine for a moment you're driving down the highway in the left lane, and you need to move over to the right. Now, with your imaginary steering wheel in front of you, go ahead and make the required motions of your arms to change lanes.

If you drive a car with any regularity, then this is likely a maneuver you've performed successfully countless times.

Yet, if you're like everyone else, you turned your imaginary wheel to the right a bit, then straightened it back out. If so, then your imaginary car just ran off the road.

It turns out that when you change lanes, what you *actually* do is turn the wheel to the right a bit, move it back to the center, then turn it to the *left* by an equal amount, and then you straighten it out (pay attention next time you're in the car to verify this for yourself).

In his book *Incognito,* neuroscientist David Eagleman presents the above steering wheel exercise to illustrate the point that virtually all the learned behaviors we've amassed over the years, and the neural networks that produce them, aren't actually controlled by or integrated with our conscious mind.

Once fully learned, the conscious mind no longer even has *access* to those networks. They're hermetically sealed off from the conscious mind circuits, and the two no longer "talk" to each other, which is why only your subconscious now knows how to change lanes.

It's also how you can perform so many of your everyday behaviors "automatically," while your conscious mind is engaged in something else entirely (your smartphone, perhaps?!). As you recall, this topic is familiar terrain.

Eagleman refers to these circuits as "zombie subroutines." Meaning that once we've mastered a particular behavior, we can perform the routine even if our conscious mind is completely offline, *like a zombie's.*

Indeed, the very goal of our learning is to create these circuits.

The vast majority of our everyday behaviors we owe to these zombie subroutines: walking, talking, driving, seat belt fastening, dressing, showering, and so on. It's their very existence that allows us grown-ups to coast through our days on "autopilot" if we wish, provided the demands of that day are like those of the previous ones.

But just what does this have to do with stage fright?

FREE THE ZOMBIE!

The process of mastering a musical instrument, as discussed in this series, requires the creation of neural networks of increasing sophistication—networks whose output results in the playing of a musical instrument.

And how do we know when we've created a well-formed network and can move to the next phase of learning?

By testing for automaticity. That is, by testing whether the learned behavior can be performed while our conscious mind is directed elsewhere. Pass this test, and we know we've created a solid zombie subroutine.

Put another way, then, the process of mastering a musical instrument is about the development of zombie subroutines of increasing complexity. Yes, the conscious mind assists in the process of creating them, through practice, but, like a parent sending their child off to college, gets out of the way once their zombies have reached maturity.

And once they've reached maturity, not only is the conscious mind no longer needed, it can actually get in the way of their execution.

Alone in your bedroom playing your well-rehearsed material, material that relies on well-formed zombie subroutines, your conscious mind is still. The problem arises when, in the presence of other ears, your conscious mind really wants you to do well. So it figures it'll add a helping hand just to make sure you get things right.

Yet, your conscious mind not only interferes with the execution of your zombie subroutine circuits, but it also doesn't even understand what to do (or worse, as demonstrated by the steering wheel exercise, has the wrong idea of what to do).

Virtually all the time-tested advice on overcoming performance anxiety centers around how to remove interference from the conscious mind. Though specific strategies may vary, the fundamental goal is to learn how to turn the conscious mind off while playing so the zombies can do their thing (or get it to attend to anything besides the *mechanics* of playing).

Now, shutting off the conscious mind, as you probably know, is no easy feat. And it's one reason why many a professional musician has turned to ingesting conscious-mind-suppressing chemicals as a means to that end. That obnoxious inner voice that's used to chattering away incessantly, narrating every second of your waking life, doesn't leave without a fight.

But the good news is there are a number of proven, time-honored ways you can remove its unwanted influence over your performance efforts.

Here are some strategies for letting your Zombie out:

DESENSITIZATION. Repetition helps. A lot. The less novel playing in front of others becomes, the less your conscious mind will care about it.

And you can do this in stages. For example, start by just recording yourself playing with the intention of sharing it somewhere. There's always the delete button. Then try playing in a spot where you're within earshot of others but not the focus, like your front porch or a neighborhood park. The more you normalize playing while others are listening, the less your brain will care.

VISUALIZATION. You can also reap the benefits of desensitization without the [real] threat of public humiliation. Simply play while imagining a captive audience in front of you. As we've discussed previously, from the brain's perspective, there's little difference between imagining doing something and actually doing something, which is exactly why it's such an effective technique.

RELAXATION. The palpitation- and perspiration-inducing "fight-or-flight" reaction that shuts down our ability to play music or control basic bodily functions is the work of our sympathetic nervous system (SNS), which is part of the autonomic nervous system. The activity of the SNS is opposed by the activity of the parasympathetic nervous system (PNS).

The PNS is active when we're chilling out and taking it easy. So, when we're performing, we want to tilt the scales toward chill and away from panic.

When we freak out onstage, it's because our thoughts have activated our SNS. In this case, our fight-or-flight reaction is being triggered by nothing but our thoughts. So, if we can break the neural connections between our thoughts and our SNS, then we can prevent our thoughts from triggering a panic reaction. Fortunately for us, having an adaptable, plastic brain makes that entirely possible!

Specifically, mindfulness practice has been shown to be highly effective at severing the link between thoughts and the SNS. A full exploration of mindfulness is well beyond the scope of this book, but the basic gist is to develop the ability to observe our thoughts without judgment. If you develop that skill, then even if you worry about screwing up onstage, those worries will no longer have the power to hijack your body and brain. Like any rewiring, developing this skill takes time, but it is worth the effort (with benefits well beyond musical performance).

Another way to tip the scales in the direction of chill involves nothing more than changing our breathing. One of the factors that drives the balance between SNS and PNS activity is how we breathe. Rapid, shallow breathing activates the SNS, which happens to be how people breathe when they're anxious, adding fuel to the fire and creating a vicious cycle of doom.

Slow breathing with a prolonged exhalation phase, on the other hand, activates the parasympathetic system, which is precisely what we want. There are many ways you can go about this, but a simple method I use is to inhale slowly through the nose, count to four, and then exhale to a count of six and begin playing at the end of your exhale. As you play, just make slow breathing your goal. This will have the added bonus of shifting your focus on your breath, rather than on yourself.

I'd also encourage you to use this breathing technique every time you sit down to play your instrument. Doing so will allow you to harness the power of classical conditioning, such that over time, simply picking up your instrument will put you into a relaxed state.

DISSOCIATION. Remember, we're all selfish creatures. Meaning, the people out there listening aren't paying nearly as much attention to you as you think they are. If you're performing for them, they're there to be *entertained* by the music, not impressed by your virtuosity. They care about the music and how it makes them feel.

So, focus on the sounds you're making, not on the person making them (i.e., you). Or focus on the musicians you're playing with if that's the case. Or the artwork on the wall. Just focus on *anything but yourself.*

The ultimate irony here, which you've likely recognized, is that the very fact that we care about sounding our best in front of others is also the very reason we so often don't sound our best in front of others. And so learning not to care so much, so that the conscious mind is quiet and the zombie subroutines can do their thing, is the key to performing at our best.

IMITATION. Millard Fuller, the founder of Habitat for Humanity, once said that "it's easier to act yourself into a new way of thinking than it is to think yourself into a new way of acting." Or, to use more recent terminology, sometimes you just have to fake it till you make it.

Why is it that actors often feel comfortable performing in front of thousands onstage, but often dread being interviewed? Because on the stage, they're playing a character. It's not the "real" them being judged out there, which removes any perceived threat to their self or identity.

Anyone can take advantage of this trick of psychological misdirection. Indeed, adopting a character or persona is a time-honored strategy that's been used by top performers in many fields to help ensure that, on the playing field or the stage, they show up how they want to show up.

Dwayne Johnson becomes "The Rock." Eldrick Woods becomes "Tiger." Stefani Germanotta becomes "Lady Gaga." David Bowie becomes "Ziggy Stardust." David Akeman becomes "Stringbean." And on and on . . .

To use this technique, just think of a performer that you admire who is cool as a cucumber onstage, and act *as if* you're them. Go all in. Or, take it even further and develop your own bombastic, larger-than-life alter ego.

BRAINJO LAW #22: Release your inner zombie to play at your best in front of others.

HOW TO ACCELERATE YOUR PROGRESS 10-FOLD (WHILE PRACTICING LESS!), PART 1

In chapter 14 you were introduced to the technique of visualization, an often underrated but immensely valuable technique, as evidenced by its vaunted position in the practice arsenal of elite-level performers of all kinds.

Beyond being a useful, portable, and cheap practice supplement, it's also one that supports the creation and reinforcement of those all-important sound-to-motor mappings that are the backbone of musical fluency. These are the brain networks responsible for translating sounds we imagine in our heads to movements of our limbs and mouth, so that those sounds are emitted from our instruments.

In the early days of learning an instrument, so much of the focus is on establishing the technical foundation for playing, all the right- and left-hand maneuvers that are required to coax pleasing sounds from our chosen music-making implement. And it can be easy to focus on that technical foundation *exclusively* for months, even years.

Until you reach a point where you realize that something is missing.

Here, in part 1 of accelerating your progress tenfold, I'm going to create a simple and effective way to use visualization to start building those sound-to-motor (or ear-to-hand) mappings very early on, **potentially shaving months or years off your progression along the Timeline of Mastery.**

Then, in chapter 26, part 2, I'll share with you another incredible practice method, one that's been shown to increase learning efficiency tenfold (and by practicing *less!*)

The basic premise behind these techniques is pretty straightforward: take something you've learned, and then visualize yourself doing it. But the specifics of what you focus on will depend in part on where you currently sit on the Timeline of Mastery.

METHOD 1: Visualization for Musical Memory Building (early stage)

For many, remembering learned material, particularly new tunes, is a struggle. I addressed this issue in a prior chapter, and there mentioned that ultimately the ability to call forth hundreds of songs on demand rests upon the creation of musical fluency. But being able to efficiently transfer recalled music to hand movements means that we're able to *remember* the music in the first place.

As I've mentioned previously, *you shouldn't attempt to play a tune until you can hum or sing it from start to finish.*

Because if you can't remember how a song goes, then you've got no hope of remembering how to *play* it. Being able to remember music is essential to musical fluency, yet all too often overlooked in the learning process.

Some folks may remember tunes easily. After hearing it a time or three, they can recall it easily later.

For others, this is not the case at all. If you're in this boat, then this visualization exercise is for you.

Here's the procedure:

STEP 1: Each time you hear a new tune you'd like to play someday, write down the title. You can use anything, but a note card works great (and then store the card in a box). If you struggle with remembering music, you might start with songs only (as opposed to instrumentals) at first.

STEP 2: When writing the tune for the first time, make sure you can hum or sing the basic melody from start to finish (not a fully arranged performance version of the song or tune, but the basic melodic contour; if it's a song, then you're remembering how the words are sung).

Ideally, have the "answer" available in some form (such as a recording of the actual tune in a playlist in iTunes, Spotify, or your preferred music player, or a recording of you humming it, etc.).

STEP 3: Periodically test yourself by grabbing a card from your box, and trying to hum or sing the basic melody.

METHOD 2: Visualization for Building Early Sound-to-Motor Maps (early to intermediate)

If you aren't one who struggles to remember melodies, then you might wish to jump straight to this visualization technique.

With this one, we'll start building those all-important connections between the sounds in your head and the positions of your hand on the banjo. Remember, these are the networks that are the foundation for jamming, picking out tunes on the fly, improvisation . . . all the things you associate with musicians at the highest level.

And, as I mentioned earlier, this type of visualization is a way for you to start creating these networks very early on.

Here's the procedure:

STEP 1: Each time you learn a new tune on the banjo, write down the title. Again, you can use anything, but note cards work great.

STEP 2: When writing it down for the first time, make sure you can play just the basic melody on your instrument. Ideally, create an "answer" in some form, either a tab of just the melody, or record yourself just playing the melody on the banjo.

STEP 3: Periodically test yourself by grabbing a card from your box, and then visualizing yourself playing through **just the basic melody** on the banjo.

Once again, the idea is to "hear" the melody in your mind as you imagine yourself (first-person perspective) playing through it on your instrument.

Over time, your brain will start building the critical associations between the sounds you imagine in your head and the movements of your hands.

Not only will these techniques accelerate your progression along the Timeline of Mastery, they're also a great way to keep track of your growing repertoire and take stock of your progress.

In part 2, we're going to dive into a bit more advanced visualization protocol, along with a memory trick to combine with it that's been shown to increase learning efficiency tenfold.

HOW TO ACCELERATE YOUR PROGRESS 10-FOLD (WHILE PRACTICING LESS!), PART 2

. . . .

It's no secret that medical school involves the memorization of heaps of information, and that making good grades in medical school is largely correlated with how much of that heap can be crammed into one's cranium prior to testing time.

Fortunately, by the time I'd gotten to medical school, I'd already developed my own battle-tested note-taking and study system for cramming large quantities of information into my cranium, honed during my preceding sixteen years of schooling.

Here was that system:

STEP 1: Write out all the lecture material (in extremely small handwriting).

STEP 2: Read through the notes, highlighting in yellow all the important stuff I don't yet know.

STEP 3: Read through the highlighted portions again, quizzing myself as I go. Highlight the important stuff I still don't know well in a different color.

STEP 4: Repeat step 3 multiple times, using a different color highlighter each time until left with only a few remaining highlights.

By the morning of testing day, I'd typically have around ten highlights left, which I'd read through in about five minutes for one final review.

Now, if you'd casually glanced at these multicolored and micrographic notes, you'd have likely thought them the product of a mind gone mad. But that madness had a method, and this system was very reliable. With it, I knew that getting a good grade was simply a matter of putting in the work.

But here's one small gigantic problem with that system: I remember almost *none* of it now.

And I can assure you that none of my classmates do, either.

The fact that I don't remember what I studied then isn't the product of some personal inadequacy but an inevitable part of human biology. It's an expected consequence based on what we know of how our brain works.

Sadly, it turns out that the best method for achieving high marks on tests—cramming—is of no use when it comes to actually retaining that tested information over the long term.

Ultimately, I did learn and remember what I needed to know for my profession, I just had to use entirely different methods to do so.

If you've been following this series for any length of time, you know by now that much of how we go about learning new things, including the conventional approach to learning a musical instrument, is typically uninformed by the process of how we learn and how our brain changes to incorporate new information. The purpose of the Brainjo Method is to incorporate what we know about the science of learning and brain change so that we learn smarter, not harder.

Perhaps nowhere is this disparity between how things are typically done and how things should be done greater than in our approach to remembering new material. Especially in school.

I'm sure you can relate to my experience. You likely spent thousands of hours of your childhood confined to a classroom desk. Chances are you too remember only the tiniest fraction of what was covered in those classrooms (likely because you found it interesting enough to revisit at some point later on).

You see, the challenge we all face as we try to continue to cram new stuff into our minds is this: How do we put new stuff in there and *keep* it there, while still holding on to the old stuff? The more time you spend learning new stuff, the less time you can spend revisiting the old stuff to make sure it's still there. So it seems that, eventually, something must give.

This is true with learning music as well, of course, especially as we continue to add new music to our repertoire. In the early going, when we know only a handful of tunes, we can practice them all in a single practice session.

As time goes on and the number of learned tunes reaches the tens or hundreds, however, things get complicated.

Practicing every one each time you sit down with the banjo is entirely impractical. No surprise then that many folks, after learning roughly twenty to thirty tunes, hit a wall. They plateau, and don't progress much further.

One reason for this is they spend all their practice time trying to hang on to those already-learned tunes, leaving no time for anything else.

How, then, do you solve this dilemma?

THE SCIENCE OF REMEMBERING

My note-taking method outlined above was a partial solution to this problem. By identifying and highlighting the information I still didn't know each time I ran through it, I eliminated the inefficiency of reviewing already-learned and memorized (at least in the short term) material.

But, like I said, almost none of it stuck with me over the long term. It was a step in the right direction, but there was something missing.

To understand what was missing, we need to review a bit about how our brain remembers things. Or, more precisely, how it *forgets* things.

THE FORGETTING CURVE

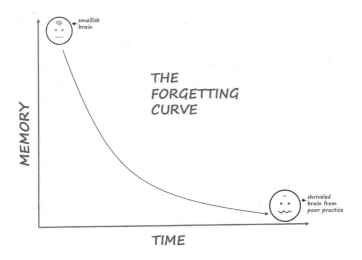

The above "forgetting curve," as the name implies, shows how a new memory "trace" in the brain degrades over time. Specifically, we're talking about something—be it an event, fact, etc.—that we deem worth remembering.

As time passes from when the memory is first encoded in a neural network, things start to get, as the top scientists say, squirrelly. As indicated by the downwardly sloping curve, the memory slowly degrades over time until it vanishes. Unless, that is, something comes along to cause it to fire again.

The best defense against the forgetting curve is to revisit that memory. But here's the counterintuitive part: when you revisit that memory makes all the difference.

Revisit the memory too soon and your time is entirely wasted; you won't increase the odds of remembering it down the road one single bit.

Revisit the memory too late and, well . . . it's too late! The memory trace has vanished, and you must build it again from scratch.

So when is the very *best* time to revisit it? Right before you're about to forget it.

A large body of research has shown there to be an ideal window of time for revisiting a memory—a goldilocks zone—that's not too close but also not too far from when you originally encoded the memory.

What's special about this goldilocks zone is that if you revisit that memory during that span, the forgetting curve not only begins anew but with a slope of forgetting that is less steep. Reviewing it once means you can wait a good bit longer before you need to visit it again:

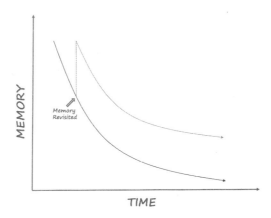

TIME

And each time you revisit the memory, you achieve the same effect, until after enough iterations the curve effectively becomes a straight line:

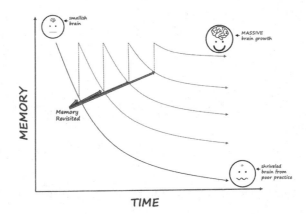

Ultimately, through these well-timed revisitations of the initial memory trace, you've literally made the memory a part of you, as much a part of your brain matter as your mitral valve is a part of your heart matter.

Since this phenomenon of human memory was first discovered in 1885 by the German psychologist Hermann Ebbinghaus, several different systems have been devised to capitalize on it, most under the label of "spaced repetition."

Spaced repetition has been harnessed to greatest effect in the field of language learning, where it's been shown to be hands down the most efficient method for building vocabulary, beating conventional approaches tenfold or more. But, since it's a universal principle of memory, it can be applied to most anything that you'd like to learn and keep with you.

And while it's true that the precise time windows are much more well established for remembering vocabulary words than for remembering music, the same general principles still apply; principles we can use to our advantage to optimize the chances of remembering the music we worked so hard to learn, and to spend a minimum of wasted time doing so.

The most obvious place to use it is in the building of your playing repertoire, especially as your ability to learn new material improves, and the amount of stuff you'd like to remember grows.

There are many potential ways you could implement the spaced repetition approach, but here's one example of how this can be done:

1. **Make five stacks of practice note cards.** Label one stack "daily," one "every week," one "every two weeks," one "every month," and one "memorized."

2. **Write down the names of the tunes you're in the process of learning.**

3. **Each time you learn a new tune, add it to your practice daily stack** (or any frequency you'd like—these are just the tunes that you know least well).

4. **Practice the tunes in your daily stack every day.** If you play a tune well, move it to the every week stack. If you don't, it stays in the daily stack.

5. **Practice the tunes in the every week stack once a week.** If you play a tune well, move it to the every two weeks stack. If you don't, it goes back to the daily stack.

6. **Practice the tunes in the every two weeks stack every two weeks.** If you play a tune well, move it to the every month stack. If you don't, it goes back to the daily stack.

7. **Practice the tunes in the every month stack once a month.** If you play it well, move it to the memorized stack. If you don't, it goes back to the daily stack.

Over time, your memorized stack should grow. These are the tunes you can count on as yours for the long haul, even if you go long stretches without playing them.

As you can imagine, this type of procedure is the sort of thing computers are quite good at. And indeed there are multiple applications available that can implement a spaced repetition algorithm (including iOS and Android apps).

With these, you just create the cards (digitally), and the program takes care of programming your schedule (the open-source program Anki is perhaps the most widely used flash card spaced repetition system).

SPACED OUT SPACE OUTS

As I said, the obvious place where you could employ this technique is in increasing the number of tunes you can play.

But I think an even more powerful, effective, "two-birds-with-one-stone" way to use it is for the rehearsal of tunes you can *visualize* yourself playing. The process is exactly the same, except that instead of playing the tune on your banjo, you just *visualize* yourself playing it through.

Since this is somewhat of an advanced technique, I'd recommend you get comfortable with the visualization practice methods discussed in part 1 before attempting it. The advantages of this approach are that you can still reap the memory benefits that would come with physical practice, while simultaneously supporting the creation and development of those neural networks that support musical fluency.

And there's virtually no equipment required. Just take your

flash cards wherever you go and you can capitalize on a proven method for making massive progress anytime, anywhere.

Then, once you've created these sound-to-motor mappings through some smartly timed visualization practice, you'll also likely find that your ability to learn and remember new material will skyrocket.

BRAINJO LAW #23: Use spaced repetition to remember music efficiently.

27

5 REASONS WHY YOUR PLAYING HAS STALLED (AND WHAT TO DO ABOUT IT!)

. . . .

If you've been at this banjo thing for any length of time, you've been there.

Gotten stuck. Hit the wall. *Plateaued.*

To some degree, this is simply a natural part of the learning process, as I've discussed before. Some of the changes that must occur in the brain to support playing an instrument take a bit of time to come to fruition. That's why Brainjo Law #13 says we should expect our progress to look like a staircase, not a straight line.

BRAINJO LAW #13: Expect your progress to look like a staircase, not a straight line.

But in this installment, I'm referring to something more than just a temporary pause in progress.

I'm referring to those times when you're truly stuck. When you feel like you've gotten as far as you can get, and you don't really know how to move forward. Or if moving forward is even an option.

Hitting this wall is very common. Masters don't make their way to the apex of expertise because they never hit that wall; they got there because they always found a way through it.

After all, studies show the greatest motivating factor for learning is *progress.* So when you get stuck and growth stalls, guess what happens next? Another instrument starts gathering dust.

So in this installment of the Laws of Brainjo, I'll be reviewing what I see as five of the most common reasons why learners hit the wall, along with a host of solutions to help you blast through it.

REASON #1: You're not inspired.

Life is full of ebbs and flows. In the beginning, you can't put your instrument down. You can't even think about anything else but playing, and you can't imagine how you ever wanted to do anything else with your time.

As infatuation wanes, as is natural, you may find yourself losing interest, and you wonder where the fireworks went.

Sometimes, this is just a natural part of every relationship, and maybe it's just because the instrument you've chosen isn't the right musical mate. But what if, on the other hand, you want to rekindle the flame, but you just can't generate a spark?

WHAT TO DO:

Reconnect with what got you here. Chances are, you started playing an instrument for a reason. Maybe a band or player you heard, a festival you went to, or even just one song. Remember and revisit those early experiences. Seek out players that inspire you. Find a festival or jam. Or, if possible, sign up for a music camp.

For me, there's nothing more inspiring than being around a group of accomplished musicians, and I always come away with my motivational tank overflowing. If you can't do the live thing for whatever reason, go on a YouTube expedition (or any other place online you like to find music), and don't come up for air until you've bookmarked some favorites, and revisit them whenever you need an inspiratory jolt.

REASON #2: You're resting on your laurels.

Once you get to a certain level of proficiency, it's really easy to get stuck in a rut with your practicing. You may also feel like you must spend most, if not all, of that practice time just *maintaining* your skills and repertoire.

But, more than likely, that's overkill. After all, there's a reason that riding a bike is, well, "like riding a bike." You can go years without doing so and, after just a bit of time to get the rust off, pick up right where you left off.

Once you've created a mature, subconscious neural network—or zombie subroutine—it's yours for the long haul. So if you practice your old stuff, do it because you *want* to, not because you *need* to.

WHAT TO DO:

Create a system for your practice that ensures you're always dedicating some of your time to new material (new tunes, techniques, etc.).

REASON #3: You're not seeking out new sources.

If all goes well in our learning journey, we become increasingly proficient at taking the sounds in our mind and getting them out into the world through our instrument.

As previously discussed, musical fluency and improvisation is predicated on the ability to map musical ideas (and the neural networks that represent them) onto motor programs. This means that once musical fluency has developed, our playing is only limited by the sounds we can imagine.

And one of the best ways to stoke that imagination, and to fill your head with new sonic possibilities, is to find new sources that inspire you.

More than likely, when you first started out, you had one or more players whose picking you aspired to. Players who were part of the reason you ventured down this road to begin with.

Be it Jimi Hendrix, Earl Scruggs, Yo-Yo Ma, or John Coltrane, it's likely that, in the beginning, there was someone whose sounds you couldn't get out of your head, and whose music you spent lots of time listening to.

And, whether you realized it or not, all that listening was a fundamental ingredient in your growth as a player.

WHAT TO DO:

Seek out new sources to obsess over, especially those with styles that differ from your own. Pay attention to the players who make your ears perk up when you listen to them and see if you can figure out what it is they do that makes that happen. If you can, learn more about their musical story, and find a way to emulate their journey in your own way (remember Brainjo Law #1: To learn to play like the masters, you must learn to play like the masters).

Build your imagination muscle. When listening to music, imagine what you'd play along with it—or how you'd adapt it—on your instrument (regardless of whether you have the technical skills needed to play it just yet).

REASON #4: You're staying in your comfort zone.

The research on learning is clear: we only improve when we practice at the edge of our limits, when we deliberately stretch the boundaries of what we're capable of and push ourselves outside of our comfort zone.

Yet, as our skills progress and the range of our automatic skill set expands, it's natural to resist going outside that comfort zone. After all, you're no longer a beginner, so why revisit those early days of struggle and slow going?

WHAT TO DO:

Embrace the struggle. Realize that the struggle represents opportunity for growth. Rather than avoid the things that are awkward and uncomfortable, seek them out because that's where the magic happens.

Break the "rules." Don't be afraid to color outside the lines. This one is especially applicable to anyone learning an instrument that's tightly linked to a musical tradition. It takes courage to step outside the bounds of that tradition, to ignore the dogmatic and vocal minority who claim that there's only one right way to do things (there isn't!). Regardless of whether your desire is to stick with that instrument's traditional repertoire or venture to less trodden lands, there's great value in spreading your wings.

Try adapting some of your favorite music from another genre to your instrument, or simply try to jam along. Or listen to a favorite musician on another instrument or even another playing style and try to emulate that sound in your style. Some of my biggest personal breakthroughs happened doing just that. Even if it doesn't work out, you'll have undoubtedly learned something.

REASON #5: You've reached the limits of your existing neural networks.

Neuroplasticity, or our ability to continue to mold our brain to suit our needs throughout life, is a phenomenal, awesome gift.

But, as Peter Parker knows, with great power comes great responsibility. Because while we can construct new neural networks from scratch, once those networks are fully formed, we have very little control over them. On the one hand, it's this transition from conscious construction to unconscious execution that allows our playing to ultimately become effortless and automatic, freeing up our attentional resources to focus on the more subtle nuances of music making.

Yet, once these mature networks are formed, and the shift from the conscious to the subconscious is complete, they also constrain our behavior (ever learned a tune entirely from tab or notation and then tried to play it another way?! Darn near impossible, ain't it?!). This is the double-edged sword of neuroplasticity, and the biological explanation for why "old habits die hard."

WHAT TO DO:

The best strategy here is one of prevention, by avoiding learning paths that create neural networks that don't suit your goals (and one of the primary goals of the Brainjo Method of instruction is to ensure that doesn't happen).

But if you find yourself unable to break free of old and bad habits, it's best to cut your losses and build new ones. Yes, it means going back to the drawing board for a bit, but in the end, it'll be well worth it.

THERE IS NO BOTTOM

When you get down to it, there's more that can be done with music than any one person can squeeze into a single lifetime. But it can be easy to miss the forest for the trees, to fall into old routines and habits, and lose sight of all that's still possible.

Keep looking for ways to grow and stretch, and this amazing musical journey will never ever end. There is no ceiling.

28

HOW TO BREAK THE TAB HABIT

· ·

Note to the Reader: As stated previously, tab or tablature is a notation system for stringed instruments. Thus, the title of this chapter could also be How to Break the Notation Habit.

In aural traditions (like the banjo), the pinnacle of musicianship, regardless of chosen instrument, is musical fluency, which I've defined previously as the ability to take imagined sounds and, via the movement of the hands, get them out into the world and into the ears of others.

The analog here is linguistic fluency, defined as the ability to take imagined concepts and, via the movement of the vocal cords, get them out into the world and into the ears of others. In essence, it allows for the transfer of information, and all its attendant meaning, from one mind to another.

The ability to do such a thing requires a specific type of neural machinery, which we build through practice. Specifically, it requires that we build mappings in the brain between the sounds we imagine and the instrument-specific movements of the hands needed to make them.

And, as you'll note, written notation isn't part of the machinery needed for musical fluency. Which means that our goal, if we wish to develop this ability, is to ensure that written notation (be it tab or standard notation) isn't baked into our core music-playing circuitry (note: this does NOT mean that written notation isn't a useful tool in the learning process—on the contrary, it is extremely useful when used wisely).

The easiest way to avoid such a situation of tab dependency, where written notation is baked into our banjo playing networks, is to take great care in the creation of said machinery, paying careful attention to the sequence and structure of practice.

Alas, this all too often does not happen. So, what to do if you find yourself in this predicament? Perhaps you've been playing for a while, be it for months or even years, and you find the idea of playing by ear hopeless, unable at this point to even envision a notation-free path to music making. Is it a truly hopeless situation?

Not in the least. The upside here is that tab dependency is not indicative of some inherent deficiency in your own capacity to make music by ear, but instead it's a natural biological consequence of the manner in which you went about learning. Barring true tone deafness, anyone—yes, *anyone*—can play music entirely by ear, provided they follow a learning path that leads to that destination.

FIRST, LET'S REVIEW SOME OF THE SIGNS OF TAB DEPENDENCY:

1. You find it difficult to memorize a new tune (memorizing tunes is *far* more challenging when they're learned exclusively by notation).

2. When you learn a new tune, something feels like it's missing. Even though all the notes are there, it doesn't sound like the version you were trying to learn.

3. You find it very difficult to make changes in the way you play a tune once it's learned.

4. You find playing a tune along with others, or jamming, very challenging.

5. You have a difficult time picking out the chord progression for a new tune.

So if some of these things resonate with you, and you'd like to free yourself of the tab shackles, then let's discuss how to right the ship.

BREAKING THE HABIT

First, the bad news. Breaking the tab habit, as is the case with all habit breaking, requires the formation of *new* habits. Better habits to replace the old ones.

This means having to take a few steps back in order to move forward again, like a veteran golfer with a 30 handicap and a swing full of compensations and compromises with no hope of shredding a point off his score without going back to basics to build his swing back from the ground up. It's not in our nature to do such things.

But it's an essential thing to do *if* you wish to progress.

So, here are a few exercises to help you get started clearing new tab-free neural pathways.

EXERCISE #1: Spend lots of time singing and humming.

When playing a tune, be it for the first or hundredth time, always begin with a "music first" approach. Start in the realm of sound, not in the realm of sight. In other words, make sure before you set about to play the tune on your instrument that you first know how you want the music you'll be making to sound. And knowing means being able to sing or hum what it is you wish to play.

The reason this is so important is because, with written notation, it's entirely possible to learn new tunes simply by memorizing the movements required to play them. By memorizing the movements, you could theoretically learn a tune from tab with your ears plugged. But this would be precisely the opposite thing we wish to do.

So spend plenty of time either singing or humming the music you play, or one day would like to play, on your instrument. Your goal here is not to become a great singer but rather to build up a robust musical memory and imagination.

EXERCISE #2: Practice visualizing.

Visualization is one of my favorite techniques for developing ear skills. Take a tune you already know or are in the process of learning and visualize yourself playing it (first-person perspective), and hearing the result in your mind.

If you initially struggle with this, then try exercise #4 below as a bridge to getting here. You also may find it easier in the beginning to start with short phrases of the tune, two to four measures perhaps (for example, you can even start doing this with your instrument nearby. Play a few measures on your instrument, put it aside, and then visualize yourself playing those same measures while hearing the result in your mind).

Do this enough, and you may find that you start doing this sort of thing automatically when you're away from your instrument (while stuck in traffic, engaged in boring conversation, etc.).

EXERCISE #3: Start picking out simple melodies by ear.

The fundamental skill for playing by ear is simply the ability to match a sound in your mind with a sound on your instrument. Unless you are tone deaf, you can do this, with practice.

If you've never done this sort of thing, just start with some simple melodies that you know very well, and work on finding the basic melody on your instrument.

EXERCISE #4: When you learn new tunes from tab, use the "Brainjo Tune-Learnin' System" to do so. Then combine it with visualization practice.

STEP 1: Learn a new tune via the Brainjo Tune-Learnin' System, a method of learning from tab to minimize the risk of tab dependency (details to follow).

STEP 2: Once you've learned the tune, record yourself playing it. The speed at which you play it here is entirely unimportant, so play it as slow as needed to play it well.

STEP 3: Play the recording, and while doing so visualize yourself playing it (you may find that you do this naturally, as you already have a memory of the recording experience to draw from).

STEP 4: Continue this listening and visualizing routine as much as you'd like, but periodically try to visualize yourself playing through the entire tune *without* the recording. Once you're able to play the entire tune start to finish without the recording, continue to practice visualizing it in this manner (as in exercise #2).

I should note here that it's probably best to start applying these exercises to new tunes, rather than ones you've already learned from tab. When trying to do this with previously learned tunes, your brain will find it all too easy to go down those well-worn tab-dependent pathways, so you'll be fighting against an old habit while simultaneously trying to build a new one. Not easy.

As I said in the beginning, the ability to play music independent of notation requires that we create neural networks that do just that. Networks that can translate the music in our mind to the movement of our hands (rather than the symbols we see to the movements of the hands).

Get started with the exercises above, and you'll start doing just that—building new, tab-independent banjo playing neural networks that will ultimately allow you to break the tab habit.

The 7-Step Brainjo Tune-Learnin' System

Here I'm going to review with you the system I recommend for learning new songs from notation or tablature. The goal here is to provide you a system for learning new tunes that:

1. Reinforces and grows the skills needed for musical fluency AND

2. Doesn't create dependency on written notation or any form to play.

STEP 1: Get the tune in your head.

One of the most common mistakes people make, which can lead to a host of potential problems, is trying to learn how to play a tune before they actually know how it sounds. The worst example of this would be to try to learn a song you've never heard before from written notation. Don't do that. Remember, you are not learning to sight-read, which is an entirely different skill!

Before you set down to play any tune, make sure you at least have its basic melody in your head.

This sort of thing is easier to do with songs, as we all have an easier time remembering melodies when they're attached to words. With a song, the rule is simple: don't try to learn to play it on your instrument until you can sing it, start to finish.

Once you start moving on to instrumentals, aka "tunes," you'll instead want to be able to hum or whistle the basic melody.

STEP 2: Learn the tune in chunks.
Don't try to learn the whole thing at once, especially early on.

Instead, break the song down into pieces, and learn those separately. Those chunks can be of whatever length feels manageable to you (which will likely be smaller in the beginning). Anywhere from one to four measures is reasonable (this is a variation of the Labyrinth Practice Technique discussed earlier).

STEP 3: Play it without the tab as soon as you can.
As you're learning each chunk, test yourself by playing through it without looking at the tab or notation. If you find that you're unable to remember it, then consider shortening the length of the chunk you're trying to learn. As you continue to do this, you will find that the amount you can remember will grow.

STEP 4: Play the song with an external timekeeping device.
Anything that keeps regular time is suitable for playing along with. The most traditional thing to use is the metronome, but anything that keeps regular time will suffice (I personally like to use drum loops that have the desired pulse I'm aiming for).

If you find that you're unable to play through the tune without the tab or notation in front of you, then go back to step 2.

The ultimate goal is for you to be able to play through the song in time with the backup tracks without having to look at the tab.

BONUS STEPS

If you want to take things even further and accelerate the development of your ear and musical fluency, then also incorporate steps 5 through 7.

STEP 5: Record yourself playing through the song.

Make a recording of your playing through the song. Speed doesn't really matter—just play it at the speed that allows you to play through the song cleanly and with good timing (if you get into the habit of doing this with every new song you learn, then you can build a playlist of your personal repertoire, which I strongly encourage!).

STEP 6: Listen to your recording and visualize playing it.

Periodically listen to your recordings. And, as you listen, visualize yourself playing through the song. Imagine yourself holding the banjo and what you're doing with your hands as you listen to the recording of yourself playing through it.

If you're unable to "see" what to do with your hands throughout the whole song, then revisit the song with the banjo in hand to fill in the memory gaps.

STEP 7: Visualize without the recording.

Now imagine yourself playing through the entire song without the recording. As you make the movements of your hands, hear the sounds that are coming out of your instrument. If you're unable to make it through the entire song, go back to step 6.

Voilà!

Note that the *only* way for you to achieve step 7 is if you've built networks in the brain that connect the movements of your hands to the sounds of your instrument, which is exactly the type of brain network needed to be a fluent musician. And a surefire way to ensure that you're building brain networks that don't incorporate written notation (even if you use notation in the learning process).

29

CROSSING THE "GAP OF SUCK"

. . . .

Here's a fact about playing a musical instrument that you should find reassuring: everybody sucks at first.

Nobody is born knowing how to play the banjo. Or the piano. Or the guitar.

Nor is the music learning algorithm baked into our brain's developmental program, unlike it is with learning to talk or walk.

Nope. We must use our general-purpose intelligence to build our banjo picking circuitry from scratch.

The wondrous thing about this is that it's possible to do so at all. Such is the gift of a plastic, malleable, customizable brain.

This means that innate ability is not the thing that matters, as any of you reading this far know by now. Everyone is capable of building a musical brain.

But building it, and building it well, is where the challenge lies. It's not those who are born with musical brains who become master musicians, it's those who are good at *building* musical brains that do so.

And arguably the single greatest challenge, the primary obstacle that weeds out more aspiring banjoists than anything else, is the Gap of Suck. Whether you make it across the Gap of Suck, or get lost in its vacuum forever, makes all the difference.

WHAT IS THE GAP OF SUCK?

The Gap of Suck, described by Kathy Sierra in her book *Badass*, is that time in the development of any skill, from sports, to writing fiction, to acting, to woodworking, to drawing, to knitting, to playing a musical instrument of any kind, when you're just no good. When you're putting in effort in practicing but have little to show for it (or, at least is *seems* that way).

The early stages in learning anything is a mixed bag. On the one hand, it is the time of greatest growth—relatively speaking, there's never another time in your journey where you'll be learning more.

At the neuronal level, this early growth requires massive restructuring in the brain. And that restructuring takes time.

Meanwhile, while all that massive brain rewiring is happening, you still suck. In fact, you may have no awareness that any progress is happening at all. From your perspective, you just aren't any good, and you want real results faster than they're coming.

Nobody enjoys this. And it's perhaps extra hard in this information age of ours. In years past, you may have only come across one or two really great players in a lifetime.

Now we can watch scores of them at the touch of a screen.

Watching a master musician can (and should) serve as a source of inspiration and fuel our desire to get better. But it can also remind us of how far we've yet to go. Or, in other words, it can serve as a poignant, omnipresent reminder of just how much we suck.

For many, the Gap of Suck will pose the greatest existential threat to their life as a musician. So anything you can do to improve your odds of making it across it is crucial to your ultimate success.

Fortunately, there's a large body of knowledge on how you can do just that—knowledge acquired from both the study of experts and of the neurobiology of learning. Here are five key strategies for making it across the Gap of Suck, all of which are common habits of the very top performers in multiple domains.

STRATEGY #1: Break it down.
Break the learning process into the smallest possible bits you can practice. Time and again, this has been shown to be essential to learning anything successfully.

Beyond being the best way to build efficient and effective neural sub-circuits, there are also tremendous psychological advantages to breaking big goals into bite-sized bits. To illustrate, consider the story of mountain climber Joe Simpson.

In 1985, Simpson found himself alone in the Peruvian Andes after having plummeted 150 feet into a deep crevasse. His climbing partner thought he was dead and continued on. Between the injuries he'd sustained and the bitter cold, making the five-mile trek back to base camp—a trek that included crossing a glacier—seemed implausible to any rational mind.

Yet, for the next three days, with frostbitten fingers and a broken leg, Simpson hobbled onward. Realizing that focusing on how far he had left to go would only serve to reinforce the terrible odds he faced, he needed to break his journey down into goals that didn't seem impossible.

So he took his one big goal—making it to base camp—and broke it down into a multitude of smaller goals that he tried to achieve in twenty minutes.

Struggling to remember how to play "Stairway to Heaven" or "Foggy Mountain Breakdown" in its entirety? Then just try to remember the first measure. Or two measures.

Not only is dividing and conquering the most effective approach to learning, but it's also the one that comes with the most rewards. The single greatest motivating factor is progress, and the more opportunities you create for demonstrating progress, the more likely you are to soldier on.

Who knows, it might even save your life one day.

STRATEGY #2: Embrace the struggle.

It's natural to equate "struggle" with "pain," and natural, then, to see your early struggles as painful. A bitter pill you must swallow. A necessary evil.

Another option is to reconfigure your thoughts about the struggle entirely.

Think for a moment about all the things that you know how to do without giving them a second thought—walking, talking, using a fork, writing your name, and so on.

Do you revel in your ability to do these things, or do you think them ordinary? I imagine it's the latter.

And why don't you think anything of them? Because you didn't have to work for them (or, more accurately, you no longer remember how you once struggled to learn those things).

If you don't have to expend much effort to get somewhere, then getting there isn't nearly as gratifying. It's the struggle to get there that gives our ultimate success its meaning.

The very best performers learn to look forward to the struggle. Struggle doesn't equate to pain. Struggle equates to *progress*.

STRATEGY #3: Set process-oriented goals.

Sure, you could set a goal like "I want to play 'Foggy Mountain Breakdown' the way Earl played it, at 120 bpm in six months."

That seems reasonable enough. But there's a problem with outcome-oriented goals that are not immediately within reach: they depend on many factors that you can't influence. There's no way to predict whether certain goals are within the realm of feasibility in a particular time frame.

Why would this be a problem? Because if you do everything right in your effort to achieve that goal but fall short, you'll come away feeling discouraged.

On the other hand, the variable you *can* influence is your process. You can control whether or not you achieve a process-oriented goal, such as "I'm going to practice for twenty minutes every evening" or "I'm going to make sure each sub-skill is automatic before moving on to the next one." These factors do influence the final outcome, and whether you adhere to them is entirely within your control.

The top performers determine the process that's most likely to lead to the outcome they desire, and then commit to following the process itself.

STRATEGY #4: Don't play the comparison game (unless it's to yourself).

As mentioned, we live in unprecedented times, with the ability to watch scores of gifted musicians at the click of a mouse or tap of the screen. And it's human nature to compare ourselves to others and see how we stack up.

Avoid that trap because nothing good ever comes from it.

When you're in the Gap of Suck, almost every player is better than you. It's just statistics. But, remember two things:

1. Everyone had to cross the Gap of Suck.

2. No matter how "good" you get, there will always be those who do things you'd like to be able to do.

If you get in the habit of playing the comparison game, then get used to a life of disappointment. Because no matter how good you become, you will never run short of players to compare yourself unfavorably to.

The flip side of these unprecedented times is it also means we have countless sources of inspiration. Those same players that you could use as a source of discouragement can instead be used as *inspiration*. They show you what's possible if you stick with this music thing and make it across the Gap of Suck.

Remember, there is no good or bad, only where you are on the Timeline of Mastery. Those players who are further along give you a glimpse of your future.

STRATEGY #5: Look backward, not forward.

We humans adapt quickly to the new status quo. All in all, it serves us well. But that means it can be easy to forget how far we've come.

As I mentioned earlier, there is no "good" or "bad," but only where you are on the Timeline of Mastery. At any moment in time, there's what's ahead of you, and what's behind you.

Combine our tendency to always look forward toward where we'd like to be, rather than backward at where we've come from, with how rapidly we adapt to any new normal, and it's easy to convince ourselves that we're not making progress.

Remember that every micro skill you've learned on your instrument once felt really hard. And, regardless of where you are, there are almost certainly players who'd like to trade places with you.

You are someone else's future.

When assessing progress, the proper metric is not how far you have left go (which is infinite), but how far you have come.

Talk to almost any expert musician and they'll tell you that there will always be more that you'd like to do, that this journey never ends, and that every position on the timeline of learning is relative. There is no finish line, only this moment in time, framed by where you've been, and where you're going.

30

THE MOST IMPORTANT SKILL YOU PROBABLY NEVER PRACTICE

. . . .

KNOWING WHAT YOU DON'T KNOW

Some of the things about learning to play an instrument are obvious.

You must know which strings to pluck, for example. Or where to place your fingers on the frets.

Other things are not so obvious.

Not surprisingly, those not-so-obvious things are oftentimes overlooked, creating hidden barriers to progress that may seem insurmountable.

Because to learn anything well, we first must know what it is we need to learn. Put another way, we must know what we don't know to understand what we still have left to learn.

It's the things we don't know that we don't know that often present hidden barriers to progress. In fact, one of the primary benefits of a teacher or a system of instruction is to alert you about the things you don't know you don't know (dizzy yet?!).

In this chapter, we'll be covering one of those hidden barriers— arguably one of the single most important skills a musician needs, yet one that many never practice.

POSSIBLE KNOWLEDGE

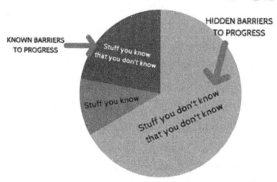

MAGIC SECRETS REVEALED

In prior chapters, I've talked about one of the seemingly magical things that a seasoned musician can do, which is to conjure up an apparently endless stream of tunes to play on their instrument.

And there are really two fundamental skills required to perform such feats of musical wizardry.

One is musical fluency, which we've previously defined as the ability to take imagined sounds in the mind and map them onto movements of the limbs so those sounds come out of our instrument.

Developing the neurobiological apparatus that allows us to accomplish such a thing takes many hours of specific, focused practice. And most deliberate practice time is spent in pursuit of this goal.

Yet, the other oftentimes underappreciated, or neglected, skill is the ability to *remember* how a tune goes.

This may sound obvious, even trivial, which perhaps is why it's rarely, if ever, touched on in teaching materials.

For some, especially those who've spent a considerable amount of time singing, it's a skill that may already be reasonably well-developed by the time they pluck their first banjo string. In this case, it usually won't present a significant barrier in their learning progression.

Others, however, may come to the banjo without a particularly well-developed musical memory. And if that's the case, you may well find yourself smack up against a wall you can't figure out how to get through.

Either way, it's something few spend time practicing, in spite of its critical importance. Those who already have a good musical memory don't practice it because they have no pressing need to, and those who don't already have a good musical memory don't practice it because they don't *realize* they need to!

How do you know, then, if this is something you should be spending some time developing? Here are some of the "symptoms" of an undeveloped musical memory:

- You find it hard to memorize tunes when learning them.
- You struggle to remember how to play tunes you've learned previously.
- You don't find it easy to sing songs from memory.
- You like to keep tabs or notation around so you can remember how a tune goes.

In previous chapters, we've covered the use of written notation in the learning process. Used wisely, it can be a helpful tool.

Used carelessly, it can become an obstruction, and this is certainly an instance where that can be true. Furthermore, we've covered strategies for the wise use of notation, including the importance of playing a tune without looking at it as soon as possible.

But equally important is to not rely on tab or written notation to remember a tune you haven't played in a while. And one reason why you may find yourself having to do such a thing is an underdeveloped musical memory.

HOW TO DEVELOP YOUR MUSICAL MEMORY

So, if you recognize any of the aforementioned symptoms, here is a suggested remedy.

This strategy has the added benefit of not only improving your musical memory but simultaneously building those sound-to-motor mappings that support musical fluency. Two birds, one stone.

In fact, even those of you who haven't experienced the aforementioned symptoms will likely find the following exercise a valuable one:

STEP 1: Create an audio playlist of tunes you know how to play.

STEP 2: Every time you learn a new tune, make a recording of yourself playing through it, and add the track to your playlist.

STEP 3: Periodically quiz yourself on your playlist—look at the tune title, and then try to recall how it goes from memory.

This is something you can do quickly, multiple times per day, even, if you wish. And, it will double as a handy record of your growing banjo repertoire.

You can also take this a step further:

STEP 4: Play the tune from your playlist, and as you do, visualize yourself playing it. As covered previously, this sort of visualizing is an incredibly useful way of building and solidifying those sound-to-motor mappings that are essential for being able to play by ear and conquer tab dependency.

Another less instrument-specific way of developing your musical memory is to simply maintain a playlist of your favorite songs, whatever genre they may be. Then, periodically quiz yourself. Look at the track title, and before playing it out loud, see if you can hum or sing it to yourself (this is also a great thing to do with tunes you *want* to learn on your instrument but haven't yet).

31

HOW TO TELL IF YOU'RE STILL GETTING BETTER, PART 1

. . . .

What's the single most frustrating thing when learning to play an instrument?

Not making progress. Or, at least, feeling as if you aren't.

As mentioned in prior chapters, progress is the single greatest motivator when it comes to learning anything. Improvement is the reward we get for our efforts.

And it's that reward that keeps us coming back.

Not getting better, or at least feeling like you're not, is the reason almost everyone quits. You hit the wall, and you don't know how to get over it.

It's a problem that's been amplified further by the double-edged sword of the internet age—access to information on *what* to play is more abundant than ever, leading many to jump aimlessly from one thing to the next without any guiding framework for the right things to work on and when, or *how* to learn it. The perfect recipe for stagnation.

One of the great challenges here is simply being able to tell if you're still getting better. Change is hard to appreciate when you're the one doing the changing.

Remember when you were a kid and people kept marveling at how much you'd grown, while you couldn't figure out what the fuss was about?

So that's part of the problem.

But even if you could observe yourself in the third person at discrete intervals, **what would you be looking for as signs of improvement**? Sure, we can tell the difference between a beginner and a professional when we hear it. But there are a gajillion intermediate steps along that path—what do those steps look like?

In the early stages of learning, measuring progress isn't too hard. When you go from never playing an instrument before to playing your first song, for example, it's abundantly clear that you've made major progress. For the most part, the technical skills are easy for us to assess.

But as your skills improve, knowing what the next step in your progression is, or where you should be putting your time and energy, becomes less and less obvious. Because if you can't clearly define where it is you want to go, how on earth are you going to know how to get there? As mentioned in the last chapter, oftentimes the scope of things we don't know that we don't know is greater than the scope of things we know that we don't know.

Identifying all the skills necessary for musical expertise and providing a road map or what to learn and when has been a central aim of the Brainjo Method of instruction. In this chapter, I'll be sharing the framework I use to help identify the obvious and not-so-obvious parts of playing an instrument.

Figuring that out has a lot to do with knowing the difference between the "hard" and the "soft" skills of playing.

THE "HARD" SKILLS

Every learned complex behavior we perform is composed of scores of various sub-skills, each with a dedicated neural subroutine that mediates their operation. And the entire reason we practice is to create those subroutines.

In his book, *The Talent Code,* author Daniel Coyle refers to two major types of these sub-skills: "Hard Skills" and "Soft Skills."

The hard and soft skills each have their unique set of key non-overlapping attributes, and understanding these differing attributes is indispensable in helping us diagnose the primary issue when stagnation does occur.

Hard skills are those that we want to perform as correctly and consistently as possible, every time (note that the word "hard" here does not refer to their level of difficulty).

Hard skills are ones you could imagine being performed by a machine, where repeatable precision is the desired objective.

Hard skills are comparatively easy to measure.

In the brain, most of the networks that mediate the hard skills will be distributed across the motor system (specifically, primary motor cortex, pre-motor and supplementary motor cortex, cerebellum, and basal ganglia).

Applied to playing music, the hard skills are what many of us think of as the technical elements of music making. Much of our practice time in the early to intermediate stages of expertise is directed toward learning the hard skills.

In the pie of knowledge, hard skills are usually things "we know that we know," or that "we know that we don't know."

For the most part, the hard skills also give us tangible signs of progress and growth. When we go from one day not being able to fret a full D chord to fingering it with ease, we know we've accomplished something.

And we know we've moved up a rung on the ladder of mastery.

As long as we have hard skills to learn and check off the to-do list, we have progress that we can identify. This is one reason why the early stages of learning are so gratifying.

Preventing stagnation in the acquisition of the hard skills is a matter of paying careful attention to the quality and sequence of practice—a topic we've covered in depth in several prior chapters. Hard skills are learned sequentially and increase in complexity over time.

The motor networks in the brain that support the hard skills are built from scratch, based on the inputs we provide when we practice. Once those networks are built, they are quite literally a part of you.

Perform the same bad golf swing 3,490 times over the course of five years and it'll be almost as much a part of you, and as unchangeable, as the color of your eyes. Which is why it's best to take the time and care needed to learn it right the first go-round.

When confined to the motor system, these learned neural subroutines may be referred to in common language as "muscle memory." More generally, we often refer to them as "habits."

And habits are the ultimate double-edged sword: a collection of good habits allows us to exploit the exponential gains of compound growth, while the accumulation of bad habits progressively constrains our future potential.

Ensuring that we form good habits is precisely why *how* we practice (the focus of this book) matters as much or more than *what* we practice (even though *what* to practice gets the lion's share of attention).

HOW THE HARD SKILLS GET YOU STUCK

With the hard skills in particular, careful attention to the sequence of learning and the nuances of effective practice are essential to continuing progress. Mistakes in learning the hard skills that lead to stagnation include:

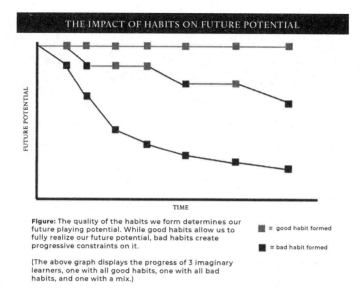

Figure: The quality of the habits we form determines our future playing potential. While good habits allow us to fully realize our future potential, bad habits create progressive constraints on it.

■ = good habit formed

■ = bad habit formed

(The above graph displays the progress of 3 imaginary learners, one with all good habits, one with all bad habits, and one with a mix.)

- Learning multiple hard skills simultaneously,
- Progressing from one skill to another before automaticity has been achieved, or
- Learning them out of sequence.

Any of the above leads to the formation of bad habits that are hard to unlearn. Usually, these kinds of mistakes stem from trying to learn material that's too technically advanced, too soon.

HOW TO GET UNSTUCK

The adage "an ounce of prevention is worth a pound of cure" certainly applies here. Pay careful attention to the sequence and structure of practice to avoid forming bad habits.

If a bad habit is identified, relearn a better one immediately (do not continue to reinforce it, or press on in hopes that it will magically fix itself).

THE "SOFT" SKILLS

As mentioned, the other kind of sub-skills are the soft skills.

As Coyle defines them, they are skills that "have many paths to a good result, not just one. These skills aren't about doing the same thing perfectly every time, but rather about being agile and interactive; about instantly recognizing patterns as they unfold and making smart, timely choices."

A tennis player's backhand volley is a hard skill. A tennis player's understanding of doubles strategy, along with when, where, and how to deploy the backhand volley, is a soft skill. Soft skills are what allow you to be flexible, to adapt to situations and solve problems that you've never seen before.

The distinction matters because, in many cases, we may not be aware that certain soft skills exist.

In the pie of knowledge, soft skills are things "we know that we don't know," along with the things that "we don't know that we know"!

And the distinction also matters because *how* we go about learning those soft skills is a different process.

In fact, many of the soft skills are not acquired through formal, or "deliberate," practice. Instead, they're acquired through the operation of pattern recognition systems that run beneath our conscious awareness.

To learn them, our job is to understand what inputs those systems need to create those skills and seek them out.

Soft skills, like hard skills, are still embedded in neural substrates. And those substrates are still created through the learning process.

But the soft skills of banjo are like *advisors* to our motor system. They help to formulate the plans for what we want to play in the first place and provide that advice to the parts of the brain involved with controlling the movements of our limbs.

For example, a seasoned musician improvising in a jam is

drawing on all manner of learned soft skills, each one contributing to what we can appreciate as expert playing, even if we can't articulate why.

Soft skills, by their nature, are harder to precisely define. Not surprisingly, they are often incompletely addressed, or neglected entirely, in musical instruction.

Yet, both the hard and soft skills are needed for mastery. And it's the soft skills that usually separate the good from the great.

HOW THE SOFT SKILLS GET YOU STUCK

There are two primary ways in which the soft skills can stand in our way.

The first is through ignorance, or simply not knowing the specific skills that are needed (the "not knowing what you don't know" part of the knowledge pie). When a soft skill stands in your way, you know you've hit a wall, but you don't really know why. You know there's a gap between where you are and where you want to be, but you don't really know how to describe what that gap consists of, much less what you need to do to cross it.

The second is knowing what those skills are, but not knowing how to acquire them. A common problem, since most instruction is heavily focused on the hard skills.

HOW TO GET UNSTUCK

The first step here is to cultivate an awareness that soft skills exist, and understand what they are. From there, it's a matter of seeking out the kinds of input and information needed to develop them.

And so, in the next chapter, we'll dig deeper into each of these to more precisely define the hard and soft skills of music making.

32

HOW TO TELL IF YOU'RE STILL GETTING BETTER, PART 2

. . . .

HOW WE GET STUCK

As we've discussed, progress is the great motivator in learning anything.

And if progress, or getting better, is the greatest motivator, then what might be the greatest de-motivator, the thing that may make you want to throw up your hands and give up in frustration? Getting stuck.

It's frustrating when we stop making progress. It's even more frustrating when we stop making progress, and we have no idea why.

In the last chapter, I reviewed the differences between the hard and soft skills of music making. Both can lead to the dreaded state of stuckness.

But the ways in which the hard and soft skills *cause* us to get stuck are very different. And for those who want to unstick themselves, it's crucial to know that difference!

SIGNS OF HARD SKILL STUCKNESS

Hard skills are what we usually think of as the technical aspects of music making. And we generally know what those skills are. In the pie of knowledge, we can divide the hard skills we've acquired at any given point in time into the skills we know that we know, and the skills that we know we don't know.

Now, hard skills often lead to stuckness. In fact, my hunch is more people give up on account of trouble with the hard skills than anything else. It's getting past the hard skills that prevents folks from moving past the early intermediate stage. For those who give up on an instrument within the first year or two, it's usually on account of hard skill woes.

And it almost always results from the early formation of bad habits, which can come from learning the hard skills in the wrong sequence, at the wrong times, or in the wrong way.

As we've covered before, it's much easier to form good habits from the start than it is to break bad ones that have already formed.

To illustrate the differences, let's review some of the hard and soft skills of banjo playing. For the hard skills, we can essentially divide these according to the mechanical skills required of each hand:

FRETTING HAND HARD SKILLS
- Fretting a string
- Fretting chords
- Pull-offs
- Hammer-ons
- Slides
- Bends

PICKING HAND HARD SKILLS
- Striking a string cleanly
- Striking the correct string
- Cleanly picking strings in succession
- Picking strings in any desired order
- Strumming

Bimanual Hard Skills Coordination of the various combinations of the above picking and fretting skills

So, in essence, the hard skills consist of an array of basic movement patterns that must first be learned by each hand, and then combined and coordinated in all manner of ways, in precise time, at will. Once all those movement patterns and the neural networks that control them have been created, however, we still must know **how** and **when** to apply them. They do us no good if we don't understand how to use them to make the music we want to make. And that's where the "soft" skills come in.

SIGNS OF SOFT SKILL STUCKNESS

As mentioned, the soft skills are like advisors to the motor system, or the conductors of the orchestra. They formulate the plans for how to use those hard-won hard skills in the service of music making.

It's in the mastery of soft skills that separates the most extraordinary from the ordinary musicians, the ones who make us rush out to buy their albums, want to learn how to play like them, or move us to jubilation or tears.

While there have been plenty of legendary musicians with ordinary hard skills but masterful soft skills, those with masterful hard skills but ordinary soft skills are a nonexistent species.

Even though computer generated music is more technically perfect than anything a human can achieve, we still prefer music made by machines of flesh and sinew over metal and transistors. Why? Because we have yet to figure out how to teach a computer the soft skills.

And, as mentioned, soft skills are the other source of stuckness. In fact, they're oftentimes an insidious, *invisible* cause of stuckness.

Why? Because in the great pie of knowledge, that whole slice of things we don't know we don't know are soft skills.

And we can't learn what we don't know to learn, right? So if you're stuck and you don't quite know why, chances are it's because of a soft skill.

Moreover, how to go about learning soft skills, even when we have some notion of what they are, is less clear.

Consider: How exactly do you know how to behave in church, an airport, at a baseball game, a football game, a funeral, a wedding, a fancy restaurant, a fast-food restaurant, a party, etc.?

How do you know how to tell the difference between a sad, happy, puzzled, surprised, angry, jealous, indignant, or constipated face?

How do you know the many ways in which tone of voice can completely change the meaning of a single word?

These are but some of the soft skills of human communication and social interactions. And the list goes on and on.

Yet do you recall ever sitting down to study or taking a class on any of these things?

Of course you don't. Somehow, your brain just figured it all out. And this is no ordinary feat, mind you, as exemplified by the fact that we've yet to program a computer that can do any of these things nearly as well as a typical human's brain.

And to figure these sorts of things out, your brain first had to know that figuring it out was important. In other words, you first had to *care* about things like the social norms in various settings or interpreting human emotions through expression and tone of voice.

Fortunately, we come wired up out of the box to care about

such things, as communicating with each other has been the key to the success of our species.

But the point being that the learning of all those soft skills itself happened subconsciously, in all that neural machinery that runs in the background. Those parts are always on, processing and analyzing sensory data to ensure that your internal models of the world are accurate, and to update them if they aren't.

Likewise, when it comes to the soft skills of banjo playing, in many instances the key is *knowing what to care about,* and then seeking out the appropriate inputs so that those subterranean circuits can do their thing.

So, then, what are examples of some of the soft skills of banjo playing?

Here's a list of some of the most significant ones—note that these are specific for players in an aural tradition, where fluency rather than recitation is the ultimate objective:

AUDITORY SKILLS
- How to separate the melody and harmony parts of a song
- How to recognize the rhythm of a song
- How to identify intervals
- How to match pitches
- How to pick out a melody
- How to identify a chord change
- How to identify a chord progression
- How to identify the key of a song

CONCEPTUAL SKILLS
- Common chord progressions
- How to construct chords
- The Nashville Number System
- Chord inversions throughout the neck
- How to transpose a song to another key
- The relationship between banjo tuning and key

- Scale patterns in various keys
- How to use a capo
- How to tune the banjo
- The structure of a song or tune archetype (bluegrass song vs. fiddle tune, for example)
- How to modify the tone of the banjo (via technique, setup, etc.)
- How to evoke specific emotions in a listener
- How to compel a listener to move
- The "rules" of different kinds of jams, genres, musical settings
- How to modify backup playing based on the instrument, singer, etc.
- How to respond and adapt to other musicians' playing

Much of these can be learned through a combination of reading (to create awareness and understanding of certain theoretical concepts, where needed), listening, and jamming (playing with other musicians or backing tracks in order to apply these concepts and generate feedback).

UNSTICKING YOURSELF—SUMMING UP

So if you're stuck, ask yourself, do I know *why* I'm stuck or not?

If it's because of a hard skill that you've habituated poorly, you may have to suck it up and take some steps backward before you can go forward again.

If it's a soft skill, consider which of these elements you may be missing. It also helps to try to precisely define your goals—i.e., what are you not able to do now that you wish you could? What is a player you admire able to do that you cannot?

33

MUSIC LESSONS
FROM STEVE MARTIN

. . . .

"I guarantee you, I had no talent. None."
—STEVE MARTIN

I think you'd be hard-pressed to name a celebrity more beloved than Steve Martin. More than an "A-lister," he's one of those people you can't imagine a world without (nor would you want to!). In fact, I hope he outlives me.

And there's seemingly no end to the things he does really, really well.

A master actor, entertainer, magician, writer, storyteller, songwriter, comedian, and—last but certainly not least—banjo player, he's clearly one of the most talented humans walking atop our spinning blue rock.

Yet, in his memoir *Born Standing Up,* he claims to have no talent. You know by now that I would agree. Because what he means by this is that he wasn't born with the skills needed to become great at all those things, he *acquired* them. He got good at a lot of things because he's good at getting good at things.

I recently had the pleasure of listening to his memoir, which recounts the early days of his career as a stand-up comedian. In addition to being entertaining, funny, and, at times, poignant, it's also an illuminating look at why he's so good at getting good. As you'll see, the secret to his success is his mastery of the science of brain change. So, there's much we can learn about learning from his story.

BRAINJO LAW #1: To learn to *play like the masters,*
we must *learn to play* like the masters.

LESSON 1: Relentlessly seek feedback and modify accordingly.

Feedback is essential to the learning process. In fact, the fundamental learning loop can be described as practice → feedback → modification → practice → feedback . . . and so on.

Increase the frequency and quality of feedback, and you accelerate the learning loop. Positive or negative, feedback is always valuable information.

Yet, most folks are apprehensive about subjecting their abilities to public scrutiny, lest they risk an unfavorable reaction. For Martin, though, bombing onstage wasn't viewed as a personal failing but a necessary and invaluable opportunity for growth.

And so he sought out time onstage whenever he could get it. His objective was never to show everyone how funny he was, but *to find out how funny he was.* He needed to know how he was doing, and who better to ask than his audience. Time onstage was an opportunity to collect data and get better, and *learning* was more important than *praise.*

Acquiring feedback is just the first step, however. The key is to then use that information to modify the thing you're trying to learn.

Which is exactly what he did. Martin kept detailed records of every joke and gag, and how they landed with the audience. He'd then take the data from those performances and write out a plan for how to make his act better the next time.

Regardless of what you're learning, the lesson here is to treat the process as a scientist would. Every practice session or performance is an experiment, a chance to test your hypothesis, rather than a referendum on your self-worth.

If the results indicate the hypothesis is incomplete or wrong, then it's back to the lab to devise a new one. Learn to love this iterative process above all else, and continued progress is guaranteed. This perspective shift is especially valuable in domains where we're prone to self-consciousness, like performance and public speaking.

BRAINJO LAW #8: There is no failure, only feedback.

LESSON 2: Seek out sources of inspiration, and study them in depth.

Martin cites many influences along his road to mastery. During his time working at the Main Street Magic Shop at Disneyland, for example, he was drawn to the act of Wally Boag, the headliner at Disney's Golden Horseshoe Revue.

But his role models and mentors were more than just sources of entertainment and inspiration. They were the subjects of intense study. Martin meticulously analyzed and memorized the nuances of Boag's routine, to the point where he could perform his act verbatim.

Nobody gets better in a vacuum, and I think it's hard to overstate the value of seeking and studying the heroes you wish to emulate, especially in the formative stages of your journey. It's no coincidence that this is a theme in every master's story.

For the musician, this means identifying the performers whose playing speaks to you most, and studying them. Study their music, study how they play, what they say, and how they learned.

BRAINJO LAW #16: Pay close attention to other players that make you *feel* something, and study them.

LESSON 3: Believe you can *become* anything.

Perhaps the biggest learning lesson in the entire book, which is also the overriding theme in all of Brainjo, is that, thanks to a brain that continuously changes throughout your life, you can reprogram yourself into what you want to become.

So getting good at playing an instrument, or anything else, has nothing to do with natural ability. That just determines where you start.

But getting good at an instrument has everything to do with *how* you learn, or how you go about reprogramming your brain. That's what determines where you end up. It's not the brain you have but the brain you build.

And this is why I loathe the concept of natural talent. Not just because it isn't useful but because it leads so many to never live out their full potential.

Without a firm belief in our capacity to continue to grow and improve, we'd never have the courage to pluck that first banjo string or hop onstage for the first time.

Nor would we have the courage to soldier on in the face of negative feedback. If our abilities are fixed, then better to remain silent and be thought of as "funny" or "musical" than to perform and remove all doubt.

Had Steve Martin bought into the talent myth, we'd never seen the likes of Navin R. Johnson or Lucky Day.

We'd have never added the phrases "I'm a wild and crazy guy" or "Well, excuuuuse me" to our collective vocabularies.

Our ears would've never been graced by the sounds of *The Crow* or *Rare Bird Alert,* and our hearts never touched by the story of *Bright Star.*

And while in the second grade, my friends and I could've never spent hours at McDonald's rolling in stitches as we tried to perfect our timing of the napkin trick.

Had Martin bought into the myth of talent, there's no telling how many millions of hours of laughter and joy the world would've lost.

34

BENDING TIME
WITH THE BANJO

. . . .

According to my calendar or, more accurately, my iPhone, 2024 has arrived. But if you're like me, you may wonder where 2023 went. Or 2022. And wasn't it just the other day we were freaking out about Y2K?

Yes, the older I get, the faster each year seems to pass by. Holidays and birthdays pile up, smearing together into an indistinguishable blur.

And I don't like it, not one bit. I happen to enjoy my time on this planet, and I know that time is finite. None of us can know in advance how long this ride will last, but I'd much rather it feel like a slow walk I can savor rather than a speeding train that leaves me struggling to keep up.

Thus far, the main focus has been on how to use neuroscience to maximize learning—ways to hack into our brain's source code to get the biggest bang for our practicing buck.

This chapter is slightly different. Here, we'll broaden our perspective a bit to identify yet another reason why this music-making business of ours is so fantastic. We'll still be hacking source code, but in this case it's for the purpose of altering our perception of time. To bring a little more slow walking and a little less speeding train into our lives.

The good news? If you're reading this, you're already part of the way there.

RELATIVELY SPEAKING

Throughout history, we humans have wrestled mightily with the concept of time. Our intuition tells us that time is a property of the universe that exists independently of us. No matter what we do, it's out there, marching forward at the same speed. In this view, time is fixed, unchanging, and regular, like the taunting tick of the metronome.

But Albert Einstein and his ingenious thought experiments demonstrated that these intuitions we have about time were actually completely wrong, no matter how true they may feel deep in our bones. Time is, in fact, relative. Even the apparent forward movement of time isn't an inviolable, fundamental feature.

So perhaps it should not be surprising that our *perception* of time is also not fixed but flexible. All minutes are not created equal. After all, everyone knows that "time flies when you're having fun."

The year it took to go from your fourth to your fifth birthday felt like an eternity. The year it takes to go from your forty-ninth to your fiftieth goes by in the blink of an eye.

One possible explanation for this phenomenon, and perhaps the most commonly held one, is purely mathematical. In relation to the rest of our lives, every minute we experience is relatively shorter than the preceding one.

For example, the year it took to move from age four to five was 20 percent of our time on this earth. The year we go from age forty-nine to fifty? A mere 2 percent.

If this is indeed the only way our brain perceives the passing of time, then there's no way out of this mathematical absolute. If this is true, then we are guaranteed to experience time as forever increasing in speed.

Of course, there's more to this story. Otherwise, this would make for a terrible chapter!

And the best part is that there *is* something we can do about it. Turns out our perception of time's passing depends on much more than a cold mathematical calculation.

LEARNING TO PROLONG TIME

When we're young, bright-eyed, and squishy, everything is new to us. We know nothing of the world around us, and must take it all in. By simply existing, our brain is bombarded with new and varied experiences all the time. Our conscious mind is forever in the present moment because it *has* to be.

And there's so much to learn!

As time goes by, however, we start to make sense of stuff, and we start to get the hang of how our bodies work. Eventually, we develop a vast library of habits and routines that carry out all the maintenance tasks of being a functioning humanoid. Their machinery is housed beneath our awareness, in the subconscious, freeing up our conscious mind to occupy itself with other stuff, should we choose to do so.

And the research on time perception indicates that it's *this* feature of childhood, this continuous barrage of new experiences and learning that is a key ingredient in how we perceive the passage of time. In studies of time perception, groups of subjects assigned to perform more novel tasks consistently judged the passing of time to be longer (in retrospect) than groups assigned less novel tasks.

Having new experiences, and learning new things, slows our perception of time. And so one antidote to time's accelerating passing is to always be learning new things.

The deck here is stacked against you a bit, mind you. As a child, continuous learning is an inevitable byproduct of existence. Loading your moments with new experiences and new things to learn as an adult, however, requires deliberate effort.

And the structure of our societies only compounds the issue. School, and learning in general, is usually viewed as something we do when we're young. By adulthood, we're supposed to know everything we need to know to make it in this world, whatever that means. As a result, it's quite easy for us to move through our days on autopilot, relying mainly on our hard-won habits, and then wonder where the time went.

But our brain's remarkable capacity to learn new things doesn't just up and vanish after childhood. We're wired for lifelong learning. And the more we engage that remarkable capacity, the longer our days will seem.

As I said earlier, chances are if you're reading this you've already begun to hack your time perception, purposefully or not. Attempting to tackle a musical instrument as an adult is a great way to make the seconds stretch. This is most true in the early stages, however, when there's much to learn. If you want to continue to reap the time-shifting capabilities of music making, you'll have to be a bit more intentional about continuing to push your boundaries— whether it's trying a new genre of music, going to your first jam, or learning a new style of playing.

Not only will you grow in the process, but you might get to savor your precious time on this planet just a little while longer.

35

TO BECOME AN EXPERT, STAY A BEGINNER

. . . .

Recently, after having received several requests for Steve Martin's "Clawhammer Medley" as a "Tune of the Week" installment on YouTube's *Clawhammer Banjo* channel, I set out to learn it. The medley consists of four classic old-time tunes Martin used to play during his comedy performances.

The tunes are played out of an open D tuning, aDAF#D, which is not a tuning I've spent much time in. In fact, while I've played the occasional fingerstyle tune in it, I'd never played anything in it in clawhammer.

The easier route would have simply been to adapt them to a tuning I'm more familiar with, such as double D, the de facto favorite for D tunes among clawhammer banjoists.

But I wanted to stay faithful to the original, so I resisted the easy road. Not surprisingly, it took a bit longer than usual to get the whole thing under my fingers.

FIGHTING THE URGE

As we've discussed in prior chapters, our ultimate objective in learning the technical aspects of music making is to take new skills that have yet to be learned and practice them to the point where they become automatic. Automaticity is a sign that a new skill has been transferred from the conscious to the subconscious parts of the brain and can now be executed without conscious effort. Any skill that hasn't been transferred to the subconscious circuitry, then, will feel effortful.

I've spent many years playing tunes out of double D tuning, and those hard-won neural grooves I'd built kept trying to guide my fingers toward those familiar and automatic movement patterns. But, of course, those were of no use. Initially, it was impossible to resist those impulses. The pull of those habits was too strong.

So learning this particular time was more challenging than what I was used to. And it's natural to get frustrated in this situation.

Then I reminded myself about the importance of the beginner's mind.

"In the beginner's mind there are many possibilities,
but in the expert's there are few."
—SHUNRYU SUZUKI

THE MIND OF A BEGINNER

In the early stages of learning a new subject or skill, *everything* feels awkward and unfamiliar. That of course includes the early stages of learning a musical instrument.

When everything is new, everything is hard. When something

feels hard, it's a signal that the brain has a good bit of rewiring to do in order to achieve what's being asked of it.

In the beginning of our musical journey, we've yet to construct any instrument-specific neural circuitry for music making, and so nothing is easy. As we improve, and as we build the foundational neural networks required to make music on our instrument, things start getting easier. And more enjoyable.

But what happens when you've reached that point of hard-won ease, and suddenly you're confronted with those beginner feelings of awkwardness again? The natural tendency is to avoid whatever it is, to go back to the familiar stuff you can do well. After all, you're not a beginner anymore, so why should you do something that makes you feel like one?

Yet, growth only occurs at the edge of our ability, when we're engaging in those very things that feel hard. How then to resist the urge to go back to the familiar? To not press on but instead revert to what's familiar and easy? By maintaining beginner's mind.

The concept of beginner's mind comes from the Zen Buddhist tradition and serves as a reminder to always retain the openness and curiosity we all have in the beginning stages of any journey. A reminder to appreciate that there's always more to learn than what's been learned, and that there is no end to the master's journey. That the scope of what we don't know will always be larger than the scope of what we do know.

That to keep walking down the road to mastery, we must never stop thinking like a beginner.

36

3 REASONS WHY PLAYING MUSIC IS GREAT FOR YOUR BRAIN

. . . .

Pro Tip: If you have a significant other in your life, particularly one who's after you to do things to improve your health, and who may not always understand your musical obsession, this might be a good piece to share with them.

Over the years in my work as a neurologist, I've often been asked the question: "What should I do to keep my brain in shape, to help protect me from getting something like Alzheimer's?"

Since one my areas of expertise is diseases of cognition—ones that affect our ability to do things like speak, learn, remember, and solve problems—it's a question I've been asked a great many times.

"Learn a musical instrument or a new language" has been my typical reply.

Most are surprised by that answer, having expected me to direct them to the latest online "brain training" program, or to the latest and greatest supplement being hawked on late-night infomercials, or perhaps encourage them to take up crossword puzzles. Yet, there's little doubt in my mind that learning to play a musical instrument ranks near or at the top of the list of brain-building activities, certainly far surpassing any of the aforementioned contenders.

And that, of course, includes learning to play the *banjo*. In fact, for reasons I'll explain below, it is *especially* true of the banjo.

REASON #1: It's a "game level" intervention.

One way of categorizing any sort of treatment or therapy we might employ in the name of better health is by the level at which it influences our biology. The highest level of intervention would be ones that influence our behavior. Lower levels of intervention influence things like cells, or molecules within cells like DNA.

And just as it's far easier to win at *Angry Birds* by playing the actual game than it is to win by manipulating its source code in real time, game level health interventions are almost always more powerful and much less likely to crash the system.

This is why the health benefits from things like changing one's diet or exercising regularly far eclipse anything that modern medicines, which operate far downstream in the biological cascade, have to offer. Though in this pharmaceutical-loving era of ours we may try to convince ourselves otherwise, we truly have no idea how to predict the full spectrum of consequences when we monkey with our source code. This is a lesson we've learned in medicine more times than we can count.

So rather than a drug we might take to boost cognitive function, which acts crudely on a single restricted domain of an incredibly complex regulatory system, with remote effects and potential risks we're not smart enough to predict, learning an instrument acts at the topmost game level, influencing the entire system in ways that support and amplify its own finely honed systems for maintaining good health. In my view, there's no safer or more effective way to improve the health of our brain than playing a musical instrument.

REASON #2: It's a "whole brain" activity.

The computational resources necessary to perform music are immense. If we measure activities that build brains in the same manner as we do those that build bodies—by total workload—then we'd be hard-pressed to find its equal.

Generally speaking, the harder you work the brain, the bigger it grows. Cognitively demanding exercises build synapses and stimulate the birth of new brain cells. Playing music literally grows brains. The more brain tissue that's involved, the greater the benefit. And no activity has been shown to involve more brain tissue than musical performance.

And while we can't be certain of the direction the arrow of causation points here, I think it's no coincidence that so many of our greatest scientists and mathematicians have also been musicians. The research also indicates that the brain-building properties of musicianship are protective. The bigger your brain, the richer the connectivity, the more protection afforded against the ravages of aging and degenerative diseases.

REASON #3: It connects us.

Most of us drastically underestimate the importance of human connection to health. But the research is abundantly clear on the issue. Loneliness and social isolation negatively impact health, down to the level of the cell.

Yet, one of the ironies of this age of communication and "connectivity" is that, in many ways, we're more disconnected from each other than ever before (no, Facebook friends don't count here). Pick up an instrument, though, and you're instantly part of a worldwide community of musicians and music lovers.

You're now a member of a group that engages in a sacred ritual where people of all abilities come together to share their music. They come together to connect over an act so fundamental to the human experience that it's found in every culture across the globe: gathering together for song and dance.

What exactly does this do for your brain?

Loneliness and social isolation, or the lack of connections with other humans, has repeatedly been shown to increase the risk of cognitive decline, increase the production of hormones linked to brain shrinkage and a heightened risk of Alzheimer's, and suppress the birth of new brain cells.

In short, from the brain's perspective, nothing good comes from it.

By contrast, those who feel well supported and who are socially connected have bigger brains and maintain their cognitive faculties for longer. Being part of a tribe nourishes and protects the brain.

So there you have it! Three great reasons why if hanging on to your marbles for as long as possible is a priority, then learning an instrument is your best medicine!

37

SHOULD YOU LEARN
MULTIPLE STYLES?

. . . .

Should bluegrass banjo players learn clawhammer?
Should clawhammer players learn old-time fingerpicking?
Should Scruggs-style pickers learn melodic style?

These sorts of questions are bandied about all the time inside banjo forums. Not surprisingly, you'll find the range of responses and opinions run the full gamut.

The argument against the proposition usually takes the same form—that learning another style takes time away from learning your primary, or initial style, thereby slowing the learning process and limiting your ultimate results. According to the naysayers, the opportunity cost isn't worth it.

As you may know, because I've touched on it in prior chapters, I strongly disagree with that line of reasoning. I'd argue that the only reason we even have this discussion at all is because the conventional learning process ends up making playing in different styles *far* more challenging than it should be.

But that's not the point I want to make here.

Instead, I'm going to present an argument for learning new styles that you may never have considered but really should. Because the benefits of breaking out of your comfort zone may be far greater than you realize.

As you'll soon discover, it could literally save your life!

MAINTAINING ORDER IN THE CHAOS

With time, everything trends toward disorder. It's a law of the universe (the second law of thermodynamics, to be precise).

Just maintaining a tidy bedroom takes daily effort.

And this battle against disorder is waged every second inside our bodies and brains, too. With time and use, things break down. Without repair and recovery mechanisms working constantly, we'd fall apart in the blink of an eye.

In the end, as remarkable a self-righting machine as our body is, disorder still eventually wins out. Over time, things stop working as well as they used to, then they stop working altogether.

That's the aging process in a nutshell.

But, if you're like most people, you'd like that process of decline and decay to go as slowly as possible. You'd like to maintain your body and brain in their best working condition for as long as possible. And you'd like as many spins around the sun as you can manage.

So now, after that bleak opening, let me raise your spirits with some good news. Because it turns out there's quite a bit we can do to slow that decline and boost the disorder-fighting forces inside us.

LEARNING TO REVERSE TIME

Recently on the *Intelligence Unshackled* podcast, I interviewed neuroscientist Dr. Michael Merzenich.

Dr. Merzenich, an inspiration of mine, has been referred to as the "Pioneer of Plasticity," having conducted much of the research that overturned the long-held notion that the brain was fixed in structure after childhood. In a number of experiments, he clearly showed that the brain could make major structural alterations throughout its lifespan.

And thank goodness this is true! Because it's our brain's ability to change itself that allows us to learn the banjo, or anything else, at any age. Without his research, this book wouldn't even exist.

But what his research has also shown is that learning new things, and the changes in the brain that occur to support it, has astonishing benefits for the health of our brain.

In one of the most remarkable studies on this subject, Dr. Merzenich and his colleagues were able to demonstrate reversal of more than twenty different established neurophysiological markers of brain aging through training alone (in this case in the domain of auditory perception). One month of training to develop particular listening skills was able to undo what had previously been thought to be inevitable and irreversible consequences of getting old.

Learning new things *reversed* **aging**, restoring the brain to a more youthful state. No magic potions, pills, or fountains required.

And the research supporting this phenomenon continues to grow. Based on the body of evidence, Merzenich believes that learning new things is the single best strategy both for keeping the brain in peak condition and protecting against dementia, including Alzheimer's disease (I happen to agree, and getting people to take full advantage of this property of their brain is a core mission of Brainjo).

RETHINKING LEARNING NEW STYLES

With this research in mind, let's revisit our opening question. Should we learn new styles, or new ways of picking the banjo? How about new instruments?

As I mentioned, the central argument given by the naysayers is that it's not worth the opportunity cost of the time you won't be spending developing your original style.

But that argument assumes that what we're optimizing for is *mastery*. It assumes that our goal is to get as good as we can possibly get (though I should add here that there's compelling evidence that, even if we're optimizing for mastery, expanding your horizons is the superior strategy).

This of course is not limited to just banjo players. From tennis to breakdancing to basket weaving, I'd venture that mastery is considered to be the primary objective for anyone developing a particular skill, whether explicitly acknowledged or not.

But what if, instead, our main goal is to improve the health and function of the brain?

What if, instead, our main goal is to strengthen the forces battling disorder in the brain, to reverse the aging process in the brain, and to maximize our protection against things like dementia and Alzheimer's?

What if, instead, our main goal is to improve our odds of a few more spins around the sun?

From this perspective, the answer is a no-brainer (sorry). We should absolutely learn new styles. And new instruments.

Because if we're looking to fully capitalize on the brain-protecting benefits of new learning, the best candidates are the things we're no good at. Because that's where we have the most room to grow.

Moreover, viewed from this perspective, continuing to work on a skill once we've reached the shallower parts of the learning curve yields diminishing returns. Once we've hit the intermediate to advanced levels, continued efforts no longer yield the same benefits to the brain.

So, if we're optimizing for brain health, sticking with one style doesn't afford us the same improvements that learning a new style, or a new instrument, would. It also means that the greatest benefits to your brain are when you're in the beginning, when your brain has yet to make any changes to support musical skill development. From the perspective of brain health, it's great to be terrible!

One final point here: if you find yourself in one of the later decades of life, you might be extra inclined to think that learning multiple styles, or instruments, is foolish. But, once again, seen from this new perspective, it is *especially important* for you. The young-uns with their freshly made brains don't have a lot of aging to undo. Those who've put more miles on their cerebral cortices, on the other hand, stand to gain the most!

38

SEEKING IMPERFECTION

· ·

I recently had the pleasure of attending the big crafty arts and crafts fair at the U.S. Cellular Center in Asheville, North Carolina.

It's an inspiring place to browse (and Asheville an inspiring place to be), with makers of all types displaying their wares of originality and artistry.

As I was walking from one booth to the next, I found myself reflecting on how different the experience was here from that of browsing the housewares section of your local department store, where you might find similar kinds of items on display.

In the department store, perfection is the norm, the product of factory-made precision. Perfection is required, and *expected*. Anything less than perfect is either discarded or banished to the land of misfit wares, aka the "clearance section." Here, there is zero tolerance for flaws.

At the craft fair, on the other hand, the pieces are far from perfect, at least in the absolute, geometrical sense. The shapes are irregular, the colors outside the margins, the round parts asymmetrical.

All of it clearly not the work of machines but of human hands.

And all of it beautiful. Here, imperfections aren't just tolerated, they're celebrated. Imperfections are a feature, not a bug.

So what do I prefer?

I'll answer that question with a picture of my favorite coffee mug, the one I drink my first cup of coffee from every morning:

Yes, I have a cupboard full of perfectly made, store-bought mugs of various sorts. None hold the same appeal.

(**RELATED**: The mug is made by Tyson Graham of Polk County, NC. At the time of this writing, you can grab one of your own at tysongrahampottery.com.)

FINDING WABI-SABI

Not long ago, I learned that there's a Japanese word for this aesthetic: *wabi-sabi*. Besides being ridiculously fun to say, wabi-sabi has also become one of my favorite concepts (not to be confused with wasabi, which is equally fun to say, but goes better with sushi).

According to aesthetics expert Leonard Koren, it is a characteristic essential to the concept of beauty in Japan, occupying "roughly the same position in the Japanese pantheon of aesthetic values as do the Greek ideals of beauty and perfection in the far West. Wabi-sabi nurtures all that is authentic by acknowledging three simple realities: 'nothing lasts, nothing is finished, and nothing is perfect.'"

While those of us in the West may be more preoccupied with perfection, we too have an appreciation and names for this aesthetic. Rustic simplicity. Understated elegance.

Perhaps the most fundamental characteristic of wabi-sabi is that it bears the unmistakable signs of human hands. Signs that convey to us that what we're beholding was made by one person, for another.

Signs that are missing from machine-made perfection.

So what's the connection here to music making?

I think it's pretty safe to say that all of us at one point or another have battled with the siren song of perfectionism. Of a desire to make what we play come out *perfect*.

Judging your playing against some imagined ideal can be especially troublesome when you're first starting out, when the gap between where you are and that beguiling perfect version is as wide as it'll ever be.

But the battle never really ends. I'd venture that the quest for perfection is the ultimate source of all dissatisfaction throughout anyone's musical journey.

Yet, here is the irony revealed by wabi-sabi: even if we were to attain that perfect ideal, odds are we wouldn't even like what we heard.

Perfect music, like perfect pottery, perfect coffee tables, or perfect frying pans, leaves us wanting. Why? Because it lacks the human element.

Because perfect music lacks . . . wabi-sabi.

Regardless of the form in which it comes, our experience of art is elevated when we can feel that it's been crafted by human hands. When it's clear that someone else made it for us to enjoy.

It's easy to lose sight of this basic fact about music—that it is something that connects us. That it is stuff we make *for each other.*

It's easy to get so focused on the details that we forget what drew us to playing music in the first place.

The point here is not to encourage you (or me!) to drop all concern for quality. It's to remember that there's so much more to music making than getting every note right. That there's so much more to the *experience* of music than just hearing all the "right" notes in all the "right" places.

Furthermore, imperfection may even be necessary. Nothing, including perfection, comes without trade-offs. In other words, to achieve technical perfection, were that even possible, we'd likely have to sacrifice something else.

Grandpa Jones may not have been the most technically precise banjo picker. Nor would he have wanted to be, as that extra bit of precision would have come at the expense of the raucous, hard-driving sound that he wanted to make. The very sound that fans love him for.

We don't listen to our favorite musicians because they are perfect. We listen because they move us.

PROGRESS AND CONNECTION
OVER PERFECTION

One remarkable thing I've noticed over the years is that I enjoy hearing just about anyone play the banjo, regardless of whether they've been playing for five weeks or fifty years. Why is that? Because technical precision is not required to make a connection.

Again, it's easy to think that if your playing isn't up to a certain level, then it's not worthy of presenting to other ears.

But that view ignores the human element. That view comes

from a conception of music narrowed by the artifice of modern musical conventions. That view misses the beauty of wabi-sabi.

When we humans began making music hundreds of thousands of years ago, it wasn't to make it to Carnegie Hall. It wasn't to win contests. It wasn't so we could score a record deal.

It was to connect with each other. It was to celebrate how lucky we are to be spending a little precious time in this incredible universe surrounded by people we love.

WHAT NEXT?

. . . .

Congratulations! As someone who's made it to the end of a book, you're in rarefied air!

So now what?

First, go forth and make some great music! Goodness knows the world needs more of that.

If nothing else, hopefully this book has equipped you with the confidence that being a musician has nothing to do with the brain you have and everything to do with the brain you *build*.

That we all are blessed with the neurobiological mechanisms that allow us to learn new complex skills and behaviors throughout our lifetime.

Make no mistake, the human brain—every human brain—is the most extraordinary object in the known universe. And you are lucky enough to have one!

OTHER POTENTIAL ITEMS OF INTEREST

As I've mentioned, the Laws of Brainjo represents the set of principles that have been incorporated into the Brainjo Method of instruction.

At the time of this writing, there are Brainjo Method courses available for clawhammer banjo, fingerstyle banjo, old-time fiddle, ukulele, and piano.

- To learn more about those courses, and to see the current menu of offerings, head over to brainjo.academy.
- Additionally, I also have a podcast and accompanying newsletter titled *Brainjo Bites,* where I continue to explore the neuroscience of learning music. Just search Brainjo Bites in your favorite podcast app or on YouTube.

Lastly, let me say thank you. The reason for taking the time to write this book is so that someone will read it, and that doing so will enrich their life in some way. I understand that, these days, there are more things vying for your attention than ever. And I understand that time is the most precious resource you have. So the fact that you've taken the time to read what I've written means the world.

If you enjoyed this book and you want to help others discover it, I would be deeply grateful if you'd share it with others and consider leaving an online review.

NOTES

. . . .

CHAPTER 2: FLUENCY OR RECITATION?

18 **humans have been making music for tens of thousands of years.** Morley, Iain. 2013. *The Prehistory of Music: Human Evolution, Archaeology, and the Origins of Musicality.* Oxford University Press.

18 **it was something we all did.** Levitin, D. J. 2008. *The World in Six Songs: How the Musical Brain Created Human Nature.* Dutton.

CHAPTER 3: THE ADVANTAGES OF AN ADULT BRAIN

22 **bathe their targets in the neurotransmitter acetylcholine.** Sarter, M., and W. M. Paolone. 2012. "Acetylcholine and Attention." In G. R. Mangun (ed.), *The Neuroscience of Attention: Attentional Control and Selection* (pp. 145–176). Oxford University Press.

22 **don't fully mature until we're in our early 20's.** Gogtay, Nitin, et al. 2004. "Dynamic Mapping of Human Cortical Development during Childhood through Early Adulthood." *Proceedings of the National Academy of Sciences of the United States of America* 101 (21): 8174–79.

24 **the speed of a typical human's nerve impulses declines by about 3% every 10 years.** Palve, Suchitra Sachin, and Sachin Bhaskar Palve. 2018. "Impact of Aging on Nerve Conduction Velocities and Late Responses in Healthy Individuals." *Journal of Neurosciences in Rural Practice* 9 (1): 112–16.

26 resulting from the combined impact of a great many factors. Serrano-Pozo, Alberto, and John H. Growdon. 2019. "Is Alzheimer's Disease Risk Modifiable?" *Journal of Alzheimer's Disease: JAD* 67 (3): 795–819.

26 **Cognitive activity.** Wilson, Robert S., et al. 2021. "Cognitive Activity and Onset Age of Incident Alzheimer Disease Dementia." *Neurology* 97 (9): e922–29.

CHAPTER 4: HOW TO PLAY "IN THE ZONE," AND WHY YOU WANT TO BE THERE

29 hacking a path through dense jungle with a machete. Waitzkin, J. 2007. *The Art of Learning: An Inner Journey to Optimal Performance.* Free Press.

30 a shift in the location and overall amount of brain activation. Dayan, Eran, and Leonardo G. Cohen. 2011. "Neuroplasticity Subserving Motor Skill Learning." *Neuron* 72 (3): 443–54.

CHAPTER 5: LEARNING WHAT CAN'T BE TAUGHT

37 after just a few seconds of listening. Grahn, Jessica A., and Matthew Brett. 2007. "Rhythm and Beat Perception in Motor Areas of the Brain." *Journal of Cognitive Neuroscience* 19 (5): 893–906.

38 machine learning algorithms modeled after the brain. Holzapfel, Andre, et al. 2012. "Selective Sampling for Beat Tracking Evaluation." *IEEE Transactions on Audio, Speech, and Language Processing* 20 (9): 2539–48.

CHAPTER 6: THE EASIEST WAY TO GET BETTER

41 most of it occurs beneath our awareness. Gazzaniga, M. S., R. B. Ivry, and G. R. Mangun. 2019. *Cognitive Neuroscience: The Biology of the Mind* (5th ed.). W. W. Norton & Company.

CHAPTER 7: FAILURE IS NOT AN OPTION

48 so that we can grow really large brains. Kuzawa, Christopher W., et al. 2014. "Metabolic Costs and Evolutionary Implications of Human Brain Development." *Proceedings of the National Academy of Sciences of the United States of America* 111 (36): 13010–15.

CHAPTER 8: HOW MUCH SHOULD YOU PRACTICE?

53 to produce the structural changes in the brain that support skill acquisition. Karni, A., et al. 1998. "The Acquisition of Skilled Motor Performance: Fast and Slow Experience-Driven Changes in Primary Motor

Cortex." *Proceedings of the National Academy of Sciences of the United States of America* 95 (3): 861–68.

CHAPTER 9: CAN YOU PRACTICE TOO MUCH?
56 one of the most influential studies on this topic. Brashers-Krug, T., R. Shadmehr, and E. Bizzi. 1996. "Consolidation in Human Motor Memory." *Nature* 382 (6588): 252–55.

CHAPTER 10: WHEN SHOULD YOU PRACTICE?
63 in the late morning to early afternoon. Wieth, Mareike B., and Rose T. Zacks. 2011. "Time of Day Effects on Problem Solving: When the Non-Optimal Is Optimal." *Thinking and Reasoning* 17 (4): 387–401.

CHAPTER 11: THE 3 INGREDIENTS OF AN EFFECTIVE PRACTICE SESSION
67 time spent engaged in deliberate practice. Ericsson, K. Anders, Ralf T. Krampe, and Clemens Tesch-Römer. 1993. "The Role of Deliberate Practice in the Acquisition of Expert Performance." *Psychological Review* 100 (3): 363–406.
73 occurs about 200-300 milliseconds after a subject has received feedback. Luck, S. J., and E. S. Kappenman (eds.). 2013. *The Oxford Handbook of Event-Related Potential Components.* Oxford University Press.

CHAPTER 13: WHAT PROGRESS REALLY LOOKS LIKE
83 like adjusting the strength of connections between synapses. Yao, Haishan, et al. 2007. "Rapid Learning in Cortical Coding of Visual Scenes." *Nature Neuroscience* 10 (6): 772–78.
83 from one region of the brain to another. Costandi, Moheb, Tim Andres Pabon, and L. L. C. Gildan Media. n.d. *Neuroplasticity: The MIT Press Essential Knowledge Series.*

CHAPTER 14: MIND OVER MATTER
87 attained simply by imagining yourself practicing. Pascual-Leone, A., et al. 1995. "Modulation of Muscle Responses Evoked by Transcranial Magnetic Stimulation during the Acquisition of New Fine Motor Skills." *Journal of Neurophysiology* 74 (3): 1037–45.
88 active during imagined banjo playing. Grèzes, J., and J. Decety. 2001. "Functional Anatomy of Execution, Mental Simulation, Observation, and Verb Generation of Actions: A Meta-Analysis." *Human Brain Mapping* 12 (1): 1–19.

CHAPTER 16: THE TIMELINE OF MASTERY (AND THE ROOTS OF IMPROVISATION)

96 that helps us learn it. Pinker, Steven. 2007. *The Language Instinct: How the Mind Creates Language*. Reprint edition. Harper Perennial Modern Classics.

CHAPTER 17: FEELING YOUR WAY TO MUSICAL MASTERY

101 it bubbles into the conscious mind as a feeling. Tsakiris, Manos, and Hugo Critchley. 2016. "Interoception beyond Homeostasis: Affect, Cognition and Mental Health." *Philosophical Transactions of the Royal Society of London. Series B, Biological Sciences* 371 (1708). https://doi.org/10.1098/rstb.2016.0002.

CHAPTER 20: WHY ANYONE CAN (AND SHOULD!) LEARN TO PLAY BY EAR

119 congenital amusia in the general population is 1.5%. Peretz, Isabelle, and Dominique T. Vuvan. 2017. "Prevalence of Congenital Amusia." *European Journal of Human Genetics: EJHG* 25 (5): 625–30.

CHAPTER 24: HOW TO SCARE AWAY STAGE FRIGHT

148 severing the link between thoughts and the SNS. Pascoe, Michaela C., et al. 2017. "Mindfulness Mediates the Physiological Markers of Stress: Systematic Review and Meta-Analysis." *Journal of Psychiatric Research* 95 (December): 156–78.

CHAPTER 26: HOW TO ACCELERATE YOUR PROGRESS 10-FOLD (WHILE PRACTICING LESS!), PART 2

160 far from when you originally encoded the memory. Kelley, Paul, and Terry Whatson. 2013. "Making Long-Term Memories in Minutes: A Spaced Learning Pattern from Memory Research in Education." *Frontiers in Human Neuroscience* 7 (September): 589.

CHAPTER 27: 5 REASONS WHY YOUR PLAYING HAS STALLED (AND WHAT TO DO ABOUT IT!)

165 single greatest motivating factor for learning is *progress.* Anderman, Eric M., Lynley Hicks Anderman, and Macmillan Reference USA (firm). 2009. *Psychology of Classroom Learning: An Encyclopedia*. Detroit: Macmillan Reference USA/Gale Cengage Learning.

CHAPTER 34: BENDING TIME WITH THE BANJO

209 than groups assigned less novel tasks. Pariyadath, Vani, and David M. Eagleman. 2012. "Subjective Duration Distortions Mirror Neural Repetition Suppression." *PloS One* 7 (12): e49362.

CHAPTER 36: 3 REASONS WHY PLAYING MUSIC IS GREAT FOR YOUR BRAIN

216 **involve more brain tissue than musical performance.** Alluri, Vinoo, et al. 2012. "Large-Scale Brain Networks Emerge from Dynamic Processing of Musical Timbre, Key and Rhythm." *NeuroImage* 59 (4): 3677–89.

217 **suppress the birth of new brain cells.** Salinas, Joel, et al. 2022. "Association of Loneliness With 10-Year Dementia Risk and Early Markers of Vulnerability for Neurocognitive Decline." *Neurology* 98 (13): e1337–48.

CHAPTER 37: SHOULD YOU LEARN MULTIPLE STYLES?

220 **irreversible consequences of getting old.** Villers-Sidani, Etienne de, et al. 2010. "Recovery of Functional and Structural Age-Related Changes in the Rat Primary Auditory Cortex with Operant Training." *Proceedings of the National Academy of Sciences of the United States of America* 107 (31): 13900–905.

ABOUT THE AUTHOR

© Jennifer Turknett

Josh Turknett, MD, is a board-certified neurologist, bestselling author, award-winning musician, founder of Brainjo and the Brainjo Academy, and creator of the Brainjo Method of instruction.

He is a frequent speaker on topics including accelerated learning, neuroplasticity, brain health, and cognitive performance.

He believes that people are capable of far more than they realize because of their incredible brains, and his work is fundamentally about helping people unlock that potential.